DO WHAT

I SAY

LIFE AS MY MOTHER

PREDICTED

BROOKE IGNET HOCKER

LITTLE
RED BIRD
PRESS

Published by Little Red Bird Press
Edited by Blake Atwood
Cover design by Damonza
Author photo by Kimberly Potterf

ISBN-13: 978-0692815779
ISBN-10: 0692815775

10 9 8 7 6 5 4 3

For my parents

And for every girl who aspires to write a book.

Go write your book.

CONTENTS

THE LOVELY LISA

"Moms are always right." – Lisa Lovely

MY PARENTS WERE SIXTEEN AND NINETEEN the day I was born. My mom had just finished eating five bowls of chili (the heartburn still haunts me), and my dad had just finished a shift at one of his three jobs when my almost nine pound, squishy baby body made its way into this world. The three of us, all kids, set out to prove everyone wrong about what it looked like to be a family led by teenagers.

As I shared in my TEDx Columbus talk, "Raising Teen Parents," my parents are amazing. They weren't your stereotypical teen parents. They're overachievers in everything. They're the center of attention and the humorous ones in a crowd. They coached and directed me through life despite the fact that we were often achieving similar milestones or learning comparable life lessons at the same time.

My dad's approach is motivation. He's a coach. He's a straight shooter. He's stubborn but emotional. He's driven and a big dreamer. He's hilarious. He's fearless. He loves hard and puts family first. He's a rule breaker at heart.

My mom's approach is confidence. She's a realist. She's just as likely to tell you you're an idiot as she is to be your best friend. She's intelligent and has a quick wit. She's ambitious. She's gorgeous. She plays by her own rules.

While we've since all grown up, bought big houses, and have landed corporate jobs where people call us boss, I have to say that some of the advice I received from them along the way seemed, well, sketchy at times. The following essays divulge moments from my life where this questionable advice proved to be valuable. Because "moms are always right," each essay opens with a piece of advice from my mother, Lisa Lovely.

ALWAYS

"Always wear nice socks to a party. You never know if they're going to make you take your shoes off."

– Lisa Lovely

Brooke Ignet Hocker

POINT YOUR TOES

"You better go if you're goin'." – *Lisa Lovely*

MY FRIEND'S FACEBOOK VIDEO SHOWED HER niece doing some impromptu Irish dancing at a picnic. The little girl is a competitive dancer, and this wasn't the first time I'd watched a video of her tiny little legs kicking and moving around to the sound of a fiddle. It was clear from the video that this was an unplanned performance. She held the hand of her littlest sister, who was trying to keep up as they danced in their street clothes on a concrete slab under the open-air shelter in the park.

Halfway through the performance, she ran out of room but just kept going. I doubt anyone without a gymnastics, dance, or figure skating background would've noticed her half-second adjustment. As a former gymnast, it flooded me with feelings of how disciplined athletes and dancers have an advanced ability to adapt while performing. I believe this ability is a competitive advantage that carries athletes into adulthood and sets them up for success in nearly everything they do.

————————

I started gymnastics when I was four years old. My parents took me to the local community services gymnastics class, which consisted of a long row of mats Velcroed together and approximately six other girls in cheap leotards from Kmart. The coach owned an official gymnastics gym but offered these classes for those that were too young to officially register or whose parents just wanted a "watered-down" version of the sport.

Even from the first class, I felt that gymnastics was "my thing." I showed high potential for discipline, the ability to listen and take direction, and all twenty-something pounds of me had the perfect build to become a serious gymnast.

Given my potential and that my family didn't really do "watered-down" versions of anything, by the time I saw the coach again I was at the real gymnastics gym for a real, serious, formal practice. Strict rules applied regardless of age: no junk food, and take supplements like bee pollen to build your immune system. But the parents' rules were stricter: they weren't allowed to watch practice except for one day on the first week of the month.

With a bottle of bee pollen in hand, my parents began the process of regular payments and carpooling to the gym while I began the routine of two-hour practices multiple times a week. By elementary school, I was leaving school thirty minutes early to find my dad out front, waiting to drive me to practice. I mastered the art of changing into my leotard while in the car and could be found running laps and warming up at the gym by 3:30 p.m.

I was encouraged and motivated by my little entourage (also known as my family) who relentlessly traveled to all of my gymnastics competitions. If the competitions were far away, we were all excited about spending the night in a hotel. And they all but drained their bank accounts to shower me with leotards, warm-up jackets, and pins for my coat. By the time I finished the third grade, I had moved into Level 5 out of 10 in my gymnastics life. This was our life as a family.

Shortly after my tenth birthday, I began traveling out of state for gymnastics camps. My dad was ten years into a twenty-year career with the airlines. With free airfare perks, the world—or at least the continental United States—was mine! Despite my parents being in their mid-twenties, they found ways to finance my tour of camps and competitions and made it known that no opportunity was off-limits. We had all bought into the idea of me becoming an Olympic gymnast, and I not-so-secretly dreamed of the day I would have my own Wheaties box photo shoot, just like Mary Lou Retton.

During the summer between fourth and fifth grade, we flew to Houston, Texas for one of many gymnastics camps I attended that year. Run by the women's Olympic gymnastics coach at the time, Bela Karolyi, the camp immediately followed the 1992 Summer Olympic Games, where attention on the sport of gymnastics had risen.

As with all gymnastics camps, we spent the first evening under evaluation to determine training groups for the rest of the week. Anything lower than the top group was not an option for me or my parents. *They didn't fly all around the country and spend their hard-earned dimes for me to be in the second-best group.* As my dad would say, "It's better to be the worst in the best group than the best in the worst group." Adrenaline combined with new-to-me gym equipment typically resulted in accomplishing tricks I'd never done before, which secured my spot in the top group. I'd made the group that all the other groups would stop and watch all week. The attention was never lost on me or my parents.

On the final day of camp, Bela Karolyi asked my parents to have a private meeting before we left. I hung out in the gym while he debriefed them on my hard work that week, my potential, and some other things they couldn't understand due to his thick Romanian accent.

As we left the camp and flew back home to Ohio, my parents shared with me that Coach Karolyi had asked if they would consider moving to Houston so I could train full-time at his gym.

Before my first day of fifth grade, photo shoots with local newspapers had been lined up and I was scheduled to be on the local news. Getting picked to train with Bela Karolyi was big news in my small town. When I saw people at high school football games or at local parades or festivals, it wasn't uncommon to hear, "Hey, aren't you that gymnast?"

After the newspaper articles and the local news spot, being a gymnast was officially my identity.

Once, the receptionists at my doctor's office forbade me to leave until I did back handsprings in the lobby. I couldn't walk by the office at school without seeing the bulletin board featuring a large picture of me posing on the balance beam.

Ultimately, my parents and I decided to stay in Ohio. They wanted a "normal" life for me and liked the fact that I was also into school activities (cheerleading). We also lived close to family, so we passed on Houston, and I stayed with the gymnastics gym I had just switched to during the Bela Karolyi hype.

"Normal" simply meant choosing not to train with an Olympic coach; it didn't mean pulling back from the sport.

By the end of fifth grade, my parents got rid of their living room furniture and had replaced it with a full-size balance beam. By sixth grade, I was a Level 6 gymnast working out four nights a week, three hours per night. My room and closet were drowning with medals and trophies, and I showed up late to a lot of parties on Friday nights, my leotard still under my clothes and bags of ice saran-wrapped around my knees.

As junior high rolled around, I was a stereotypical gymnast who was too flat-chested to need a bra, but I wore one because everyone else did. My period was still years away. I was a Level 7 gymnast and began working out five days a week, four hours per night. If there were tricks or routines that needed shaping up, it wasn't uncommon for my parents to pay for a private lesson on a Sunday or to take me to the local playground where there was plenty of grassy space for me to practice my floor routine.

I knew the names of popular classical songs that could be used for floor music, and I wore my hair like Olympic gymnast Shannon Miller at every competition. I made As and Bs at school, but homework was always an afterthought with my parents. They often said, "You could probably finish that in the morning," or they'd ask, "Do you think you have time to just do it in study hall tomorrow?" I became a pro at balancing the demands of school and gymnastics in a way far beyond my years. Even before my braces came off, I had perfected the art of negotiating my time with a full schedule.

Out of a ten-point scale, I started scoring nines in competitions on the beam and in floor routines. I'd normally land in first or second place in those events. I was labeled as "graceful" and put a lot of energy into choreographing my routines. I was competing locally, regionally, and nationally. Trips to Florida for my family always centered on a competition.

By high school, I was a Level 9 gymnast. My parents watched me behind a glass window at the gym. We became experts at reading each other's facial expressions even when our expressions seemed non-existent to others. I always knew when they were proud or frustrated with what they were seeing in my training, and they always knew when fear was settling in on a certain event or when my confidence was carrying me through the night's practice.

My dad would coach me to stand with my hands on my hips because it made me look more confident. My mom would spray a half-bottle of hairspray on my bun before each competition. My gym bag was my prized possession, and an evening didn't exist where chalk wasn't covering my hands and thighs while I sat icing my injuries.

My parents rallied around my gymnastics, even when they were going through a divorce. Gymnastics sparked fights among us, often born out of my fear of throwing certain tricks. Gymnastics had me listening to cassette tapes of a sports psychologist before every competition. Gymnastics made my friends and family so proud of me.

Gymnastics was life.

––––––––

When you're in an intense sport, and specifically an individual sport, it's the best character training a person can get. Besides the obvious benefits— discipline, hard work, and healthy bodies—sports like gymnastics, dance, and figure skating can mold a person for life, influence the way they behave, and affect the choices they'll make as a working adult.

Disciplined athletes have been trained their entire lives on how to receive coaching, how to look people in the eye when they're talking to them, how to perform when it's time, how to deal with pressure and stress, how to overcome mental and physical injuries, how to go the extra mile, how to balance everything, how not to be intimidated by others, how to read a room of people judging them, course-correct when needed, and how to push their own limits despite standing face-to-face with fear.

––––––––

As I watched my friend's niece receive applause

for her Irish dance, I knew her secrets. I knew about the injuries and the tears and the trophies. I knew she somehow found her parents in the crowd and was likely feeding off their nonverbal coaching. I knew she ran out of space to dance on that concrete slab but kept dancing anyway. I knew she probably had homework she hadn't finished yet but would manage to get it done in the morning. I knew she had likely put in over twenty hours' worth of practice that week. I knew all of this would make her successful when she grew up.

WHAT IF THEY THINK I'M DUMB?

"They put their pants on one leg at a time, just like we do."

– Lisa Lovely

N O ONE REALLY KNOWS WHO THE infamous "they" are, but we sure do spend a lot of our time trying to please them, or trying to hide our talents and vulnerabilities from "they."

I have talents. I'm a writer and a blogger. I'm funny and have often wondered if I could do stand-up comedy. I'm a good dancer and have talents in choreography. I'm a natural-born therapist. I inspire people. I'm a good speaker. I'm creative and decent at drawing (well, kind of). I could probably write a TV script or funny short film, and I'd like to believe I could act in them too. I think I'd be a great psychology or sociology professor. And I'd make a great life coach, even though my friends say that's not a real job.

But I would never tell anyone these things. *What if they think I'm dumb?*

I was fortunate to grow up with parents who instilled a lot of confidence in me on a daily basis. On more than one occasion, my dad has told me, "You go in there and tell them . . . " followed by a list of my accomplishments or some fancy way to phrase that I'm a dedicated, reliable, hardworking person, and it's their loss if they don't hire me, friend me, or include me on that particular opportunity. My mom has a tendency to say "Psh" and wave her hand in the air to symbolize, "They have nothing on you. Are you serious?" Because life, to her, is clearly all one big competition among one another, and specifically among women.

My parents have always served as confidence cheerleaders, and I've unintentionally (or subconsciously intentionally) surrounded myself with friends who do the same. At age nineteen I even got a tattoo on my hip that means "confidence." I was obviously having an overly confident day then.

Unfortunately, no permanent ink can erase the curse of "What if they think I'm dumb?" Personally, I have arenas in which I know "they" won't think I'm dumb. If "they" think I'm dumb, then I'll think they're stupid (similar to what a five-year-old would do). Those moments typically come in the form of my day job or an arena in which others consider me an expert. Oftentimes, they're things I don't even really want to be an expert in, like Excel spreadsheets, the best way to paint a room, directions to a downtown restaurant, or the type of water softener the neighbor should buy, but life just happens that way. They're typically things I could rally up enough troops behind me (isn't that what we do when we're trying to prove a point?) to say "Yeah, she *does* know what she's talking about . . . and *you're* the dumb one."

When you worry about what others will think of you, it's most often about the things you'd describe with words like "passion," "desire," or "dream."

In 2015, I started a blog with a friend called *Gals with Goals*. We decided to each try something new every month of the year and blog about what we learned along the way. It existed to fill the void in our lives after we had accomplished our educational and professional goals while we swam in the "Are we supposed to have kids now?" phase of our lives. I was in love with the blog idea before the site even launched. I have a bad habit (I like to call it an "amazing talent") of falling hard in love with my own ideas. So, we each determined our list of goals for the year, we posed for a photoshoot where neither of us looked good in the same picture, and we committed to blogging every three or four days for 365 days.

The site went live on January 1, 2015. *We were exposed*. We had granted one free daily admission for every "they" out there to criticize us for the next year. I got a nervous feeling in my stomach just thinking about the judgment we'd face. I had already created a mental Rolodex of people who would hate the idea and hate my writing—which obviously meant they would hate me too.

I had a short stint of blogging in college with my only real reader being a friend of mine from high school. He had told me for years that I should write a book or start another blog. So here I was, approximately fifteen years later, starting another blog. Only now I was in my thirties and had a real job that required the occasional suit jacket. Thanks to my plan to share all my blog posts on Facebook, my potential readers stretched from executives at a Fortune 100 company to long-lost sixth-grade boyfriends who had known me when bangs and hairspray were my life.

What if they think I'm dumb?

As I started to post, I tailored my writing style to keep in mind the diverse group of people who may read it. I used humor, but I wasn't all in like I had hoped to be. Every time I shared a post, I would cringe while waiting to see my first "like," which typically came from my aunt or an old high school friend. After a few likes, I'd receive a few comments: "Great blog!" "You're so funny!" "You're so inspiring." With every word of affirmation, I wrote more as my real self. I typed more like I talked. I blogged in a similar way to how I spoke with close friends and less how I talked in formal meetings at work. When I worked my way through a goal of waking up early to work out, I posted selfies of what I looked like at 4:45 a.m. People loved it! Literally, they commented with, "I love this," or, "I love you."

"They" loved me—*the real me!*

I received private messages, emails, and texts from friends who said they loved my blog. People at work caught me in the hallways and asked me how my goals were going. When goals resonated with people, they would tell me about their experiences doing something similar, or give me tips on how to do it better, or they'd tell me I was crazy yet inspiring. *I was inspiring.* Some even said they were trying the goals I was writing about simply because I was writing about them.

I was doing it. I was me and they were suddenly not the "they" I had feared.

They didn't think I was dumb.

As the months went on, there were a couple busy weeks where I let four or five days lapse before I posted again due to my schedule. During these times, "they" were asking me when I was going to post again, as if they were waiting on the edge of their seats for something I had hidden for so long.

My confidence grew to a point that I actually considered another tattoo.

After six months of blogging, I felt like I was finally letting the world see the real me. It took a long list of crazy goals and writing about the highs and lows of each one to get to that place. I was finally inviting "they" to see my pictures, my writing, my humor, my thoughts, my successes, and my failures . . . and it felt really good. I felt like I could pretty much do anything because I was less concerned with what "they" would think of me.

So why do we wait and not dive headfirst into what we really want to do? Why do we quietly please "them"? Is it just so we don't have to face criticism? Is it because it's easier? Is it because we don't have enough confidence, *tattoo or not*, to follow through? I missed out on fifteen years of writing and blogging because I thought "they" would think I was dumb.

I've noticed that we oftentimes see others' accomplishments which we know took some level of bravery to ignore "them," and we respond in one of two ways:

1. We praise them because we know they're facing a certain circumstance. We cheer them on through a chronic illness or a divorce. We admire them as they start a company, write a book, or pursue a creative calling. We tell our friends their stories and how the odds were against them, but they're rising above it. We may even donate to their campaigns or buy their artwork to show our support.

2. We hate them. They stole *our* idea. They're doing what we always wanted to do and they're likely doing it worse than what we would've done (or they're doing it better, which is really the worst!). This option comes with a lot of responsibilities in the gossip department. We gather our closest friends and family who will agree with us on their flaws. We have now become the "they" and perpetuated the cycle.

Let's stop holding ourselves back because of what others may think. Let's stop fearing that an imaginary "they" will judge us. Let's stop waiting until the odds are against us to finally rise up and show our talents. Let's not become a "they" ourselves and invest too much energy in criticizing risk takers. Let's break up with "they" for good.

I hear they're dumb anyway.

THE WAR ON CUTE MILLENNIALS

"Someday they'll hire someone younger and prettier than

you and you'll hate her just because." – Lisa Lovely

Dear Millennial in the Michael Kors Boots,

You know, I could have those boots if I wanted. I mean, I've been busy working sixty hours a week and doing laundry and paying bills and other grown-up things, and I'm typically too exhausted to go shopping after work—but I could if I wanted. I realize you knew the wedge boot was trendy before I did, but I can't say I haven't pinned a couple pictures of boots that look similar on my Pinterest board on Friday nights when I eat large pizzas by myself. I know you felt proud when your boots transformed from a day to night look last week when we all went to that networking event in the evening. What a blast.

Sincerely,
Flats

———————

Dear Guy Born in 1990,

I realize we bonded over fitness and protein shakes
and all things gym-related when we became friends.
It's been great conversation and inspiring on some
level. I just want to thank you for that and for the
gentle reminder that I am no longer the fitness star I
once was before I turned thirty. It feels amazing to
hear about your workouts and know that I left work
and binged on bread at the Cheesecake Factory
before they brought out my shareable-size pasta while
I dined alone. I especially feel inspired when I have a
hard time buttoning my dress pants in the morning
but know that you will be sore from last night's
workout when I see you again.

Sincerely,
Diet Starts Monday

———————

Dear Wavy Hair Girl,

Just because my hair is in a mid-afternoon "I-work-
too-much" bun doesn't mean my hair couldn't look
like yours with the perfect beach wave. Maybe I like a
bun.

Sincerely,
Librarian Look

————

Dear Class of 2016,

Don't forget to look up from that phone every once in awhile.

Sincerely,
I Had a Pager at Your Age

————

Dear Girl in the Dressing Room Next to Me,

Hearing you yell over the dressing room door to your friend to let her know that you're swimming in a size 8 dress is amazing. When you said that you couldn't even believe the sales girl would give you a size that big was great too. I was so sad for you when I heard they would have to special order your size because you're so tiny. Poor baby. How will you deal?

Sincerely,
Size 8 on a Good Day

————

Dear Intern in the Five-Inch High Heels,

I don't want to say it brought me pleasure to see you struggling to walk during your building tour orientation, but . . .

Sincerely,
Tour Guide

———————

Dear Barbie Girl,

Your lip gloss and perfect pony-tail at the gym has got to stop. It has to stop now. If I keep seeing it, I'm going to start wearing more make-up to the gym to keep up and I don't have the time to dedicate to this nonsense. Just be ugly for a day, would ya?

Sincerely,
Crying in the Locker Room

———————

Dear Intern Who Parks Four Blocks Away,

That's not me who is driving by you in the mornings and not offering you a ride. Twenty-five degrees isn't really that cold for Ohio anyway.

Sincerely,
Priority Parking

THIRTY LOVE LETTERS IN THIRTY

DAYS

"Always call people by their first name when you see them.

They'll like you more, and that's how you become prom

queen." – Lisa Lovely

O NCE MY BEST FRIEND ANGELA
AND I arrived in our thirties, most of our
birthday dinners turned into a carbohydrate
binge followed by too many tears. We had
seemingly accomplished every graduate level degree
and professional goal we had set for ourselves, but
still felt the void one feels when they haven't decided
if they want to have kids and the excitement of work
drowns in the face of the daily commute.

After an overpriced brunch and a couple hours of

brainstorming, we decided to spend 2015 trying one new goal per month for the entire year. We would try things that made us face our fears, that we were curious about, that made us healthier, or that we always wanted to do but always found ways to procrastinate. To keep us honest, we committed to blogging about our experiences every few days.

We toasted to a new year and each created a list of twelve goals for the twelve months ahead.

For our first goals, I woke up before the sun to work out while Angela ate vegan. As the months went on, I tried a new recipe every day while Angela prepared for European travel. I tried to eliminate complaining while Angela did yoga. I took singing lessons while Angela read every day. We were doing everything we had set out to do and were gathering a tribe of blog followers along the way.

As the weather in Ohio danced between spring and summer, I was buried in stationery, pens, and stamps for my goal the following month. I was going to spend thirty days writing love letters to the people in my life who had deeply impacted me but to whom I mostly communicated with through likes on their Facebook photos.

I wanted to reach the people I quietly cheered for when I saw they'd hit a milestone to be celebrated but who I tended to just generically comment, "Congrats!" on their Instagram photos. I also wanted to reach those I distantly wept for when I saw that tragedy had struck but seldom reached out because I couldn't find the right words to say. And I was determined to reach the people who had been telling me for the last twenty years, "We should get together next time you're in town."

Before I dove into letter-writing, I had just exited a season of life where I had attended a long string of weddings and funerals. I noticed that every time I received a perfectly pressed invitation or read a newspaper write-up, I saw the full formal name of the person I'd soon be celebrating or honoring.

I attended these celebrations feeling emotionally connected to the person, but I'd just stare at the paper and realize I never knew their middle name until that moment. I realized that I never knew the friend's formal name was actually Christopher even though I'd called him Adam his whole life. Or that Elizabeth was actually her middle name and Jane was her first name, which matched her mother's name. Or his name ended with Jr. and he had the same first name as his grandfather. Or that they were born in an era where it was common to not even have a middle name. I felt like I knew these friends but had somehow betrayed them for never really knowing their real birth names.

As I started writing letters, I addressed each one with the person's full formal name, even including maiden names for the ones who were married or resurrecting middle names that had been changed following their weddings. I signed my name the same way using all four of my names: first, middle, maiden, married. I wanted to let the letter recipients know that I saw them, I knew them, and I respected them. I wanted to reach them on a personal level that recognized the name their mother had given them.

I started waking up at 5:00 a.m. to write these letters. I stayed up past midnight to write these letters. I sat in the sun on my patio to write these letters. I stayed in the hotel room on vacation to write these letters. I carried stationery in my purse at all times in case I felt a wave of thoughts, memories, and love for a person on my list of pen pals.

With every letter I wrote, a steady stream of tears would flow down my face. I loved these people from the bottom of my soul, but suddenly realized I had never shared those words on my paper with them.

I wrote to my great-grandparents, my high school girlfriends, my old next-door neighbor, a college roommate, a best friend's four-year-old daughter, an old coworker, my husband's best friend's wife, an aunt, my stepmom, an uncle, my mom's best friend, and to a friend who lived in an RV and didn't even have a permanent address.

With every letter I crafted, I included an introduction to let them know they often crossed my mind and they were so deeply loved. I shared the top ten things that came to mind when I thought of them. I wrote about instances that made me laugh even twenty years later. I wrote what I admired about them that I had assumed they always knew. I wrote compliments about their physical appearance and how they were flawless through my eyes. I made scribbles when I misspelled words, my words and lines slanted to the right, and I smeared the ink thanks to my left-handedness, *but I kept writing*.

I told my stepmom how I appreciated her in ways I'd never told her before. I told girlfriends how I admired them for becoming nurses. I told my father-in-law how thankful I was that he had raised my husband to be the man he is today. I told my friend's daughter how I hoped she would get a lot of gifts for her fifth birthday. I told my Grandma how she's a great daughter to her parents. I told people how I saw them, *the whole them*.

Day after day I would cry my way through letters and post pictures and highlights about the person on the blog. I included antics about how I met them or what I admired about them the most. I would simultaneously send the letters through snail mail and pray they were delivered and well-received on the other end.

After about a week, I started to receive text messages from people saying they had gotten my letters. They said it made them cry and made them miss me. They said they loved my blog and shared it with their families. They would comment on the outdated pictures I was using online and continue the cycle of saying they hoped we would get together soon.

Maybe life is meant to be a coffee date waiting to happen.

After a couple weeks, my Facebook private message inbox was full of notes from the latest letter recipients telling me how they were so touched that I had seen those positive traits in them. They would compliment me back and tell me I was sweet.

By the third and fourth week, I was getting tagged on social media posts by my letter recipients who said I had made their day, their week, and their month. Some said they'd hung the letter up on their refrigerators and had let their spouses and parents read it. They were leaving me voicemails or pulling me aside at get-togethers to say how the letter was so unexpected.

By the time the month wrapped, I was emotionally exhausted. I had laid my heart out on thirty pieces of paper with thirty envelopes and thirty stamps. I felt vulnerable, exposed, and tired. I was still deciding how I felt about everyone responding to me on social media after I had spent the time to handwrite a note to them.

The line between selflessness and selfishness can get fuzzy at times.

As the thirty days came to a close, I moved on to my next goal. I wrote the letter-writing off as a good deed and free pass into Heaven someday.

Three weeks later, someone wrote me back—in ink, on a letter.

I pulled an envelope out of the mailbox and opened it to find a letter from my aunt who lives on the other side of the country. She wrote some of the same words others had been texting, but it was in her handwriting and had traveled from Colorado to Ohio to get to me.

She reminded me how I used to love getting candy eyeballs on my ice cream cones at Dairy Queen, and she said how beautiful I was on the day of my wedding. Her handwriting was familiar and slanted with the same left-handed flare as mine. I felt so loved that all I could do was pace around the house and cheerfully share the news with my friends that someone wrote me back, even if that someone was related to me.

Two weeks later, someone else wrote me back—in ink, on a letter.

I pulled an envelope out of the mailbox and it was addressed to me with my full formal name: Brooke Nichole Ignet Hocker. I felt like someone knew me on a secret personal level, all the way down to the often left out "h" in my middle name. The letter was from a college friend.

She mimicked my letter format and told me ten things that came to mind when she thought of me. While I had created the idea, it suddenly looked foreign and exciting to me on the paper while perfectly flowing with the combination of her print and cursive writing.

She told me how she loved my sense of style, which I had never known her to notice about me. She told me I was an amazing storyteller, which eased the embarrassment I'd felt from sometimes talking her ear off. She told me that she would be thrilled if her daughter grew up to be just like me.

I read it ten times and cried eleven. She knew me—and all four of my names.

Brooke Ignet Hocker

EIGHTY-EIGHT FORTUNES

"Get in, get up, and get out." – Lisa Lovely

AS MY FRIEND JOHN WOULD SAY, gambling has always been Plan A as far as income and success is concerned for me and my family. Although we have real, grown-up corporate jobs that pay us well and require us to dress up and boss people around, we still believe that a slot machine jackpot, a million-dollar scratch-off instant lottery ticket, or a perfectly matched mega-million ticket is really our lives' destiny. Until we win that money, we will spend every Thanksgiving downing mashed potatoes and pumpkin pie while we play "What would you do if you won a million dollars?"

If there's ever a new member of the family who joins us—say a cousin brings home a new date or an in-law decides to invite a sibling who's technically not related to us—we'd bully the new pseudo-family member if they responded with, "I have no idea what I'd do if I won that much money." We've all been dreaming for years about the houses, cars, and unnecessary life-size pieces of art we'd buy while simultaneously crafting the list of people to whom we'd like to give money (this also includes the short list of people we'd screw over because they screwed us over at some point in our lives). We really can't understand how others do not plan for such things too.

When I turned twenty-one, the only thing on my mind was going to the casino. My mom and I had talked about it for years, and it was her goal in life to introduce me to (the addiction of) slot machines. So the stars aligned when my birthday fell on the week of Spring Break during college, and off my mom, Grandma, and I went to Argosy Casino in Indiana. We each had one hundred dollars in our pocket, and I had a new, shiny license to flash upon entering.

I quickly fell in love with the idea of it all now that I was old enough to legally gamble. My parents had been buying me scratch-off instant lottery tickets since I had braces, but now I was putting my own grown-up money into a machine, pushing a button, and waiting for it to pay me enough money to buy the twelve-bedroom, fourteen-bath home I so desperately needed.

At that time, the only slot machines available at the casino ranged from twenty-five cents to one dollar, and all of them operated as a set of reels. You'd put your money in, you'd no longer be able to calculate how many quarters were in a dollar because all elementary math skills you once had were gone, you'd either push the button or pull the lever on the side, and then you would wait as each reel would land one-by-one, *also known as an eternity*. The majority of the machines were "Lucky 7s" or "Double Diamonds," and you'd occasionally see one with a fun theme that played music while it spun. *Throw a machine on the floor that has pictures of hot tamales on it that light up when you match three jars of hot sauce and I'll give you all that's in my checking account, and likely my savings too.*

After my initial casino adventures, I returned to college and finished out my degree (Plan B) and used most summer and holiday breaks as an excuse to hit the casino with one of my parents. (None of my friends could understand this new gambling world of mine. They kept saying phrases like, "But couldn't you buy new clothes or something fun with the money?" Amateurs.). My mom and her best friend Joy would always come up with some great excuse of why we had to go that seemed acceptable to their husbands. It wasn't uncommon for my mom to call her best friend's husband and ask him if he minded if they went to the casino, saying phrases like, "I haven't even talked to Joy, but thought I'd run it by you first." Meanwhile, Joy would be sitting in the car next to her. It always worked. My mom's car could almost drive itself to and from the casino at that point.

Over the years, the casino started to offer penny slots. They were more video-style games, which meant they were *way* more entertaining and included music and dancing characters, like smiley faces with hands who would come down and surprise you with additional winnings while 1950s jazz played in the background, or little cartoon men who would go into a virtual cave and dig for gold when you'd match the scattered images. You could bet thirty lines at a time, but at a penny each, you were only playing five cents more than you would be playing on one line at a twenty-five-cent machine. Plus, you had far greater odds of dancing animated characters making your dreams come true.

The penny slots served as a great backup option when one of us got down to our last twenty or forty dollars because, inevitably, another one of us was on a hot streak. *And you don't want to be the stick-in-the-mud friend or family member who wants to leave while everyone else is winning or you'll be banished from casino trips for all of eternity. You are to magically make your final ten dollars last the rest of the evening until everyone is ready to leave.*

Shortly after Ohio passed a law that would allow casinos to start going up close to home, I finally had the chance to graduate to the big leagues and take my gambling show on the road to Las Vegas. I don't know what type of calling-each-other's husbands they had to do to get that trip in the books, but Joy, my mom, and I made the four-hour flight and gave every penny we had on us to every slot machine we could get our tiny little hands on. It was glorious . . . *up until we flew home and couldn't even pay cash for a cup of coffee in the airport.*

Following a couple trips to Vegas with my mom, my husband Chris started attending a yearly work conference in Sin City. I hated being the tagalong wife to any function, and mainly when no other wives were going. However, I also hated the idea of being one of many wives crowded in the corner chatting about nonsense and trying to silently one-up each other with great hair and stylish outfits. But when Vegas is involved, I'll be that wife. No other wives were going to Vegas for that conference. (Thank goodness. What if they were the type who didn't know what they'd do with a million dollars?!) But I had no reservations about booking a plane ticket and crashing the hotel room that my husband's company would be covering.

With every Vegas trip I made, whether with my mom or with Chris, I'd have a few days of losing money, a day or two of winning money, and an in-between day where I'd lose a little money but stalled it a bit by shopping or hitting the pool to distract myself from the slot machines. Around five hundred dollars was about the most I had ever cashed out on a ticket from a slot machine, which was traditionally just winning some of the money back I had lost the day before.

When I traveled with my mom, I would always come back broke. When I traveled with Chris, I would always come back with at least half of what I took.

Your risk level really changes with a joint bank account.

By 2015, I had approximately ten trips to Vegas and hundreds of trips to the local casinos under my belt. I had yet to win a jackpot, or even half of a jackpot, but the hope of life being changed by one dancing animated character or cartoon-style Michael Jackson while "Thriller" played in the background and people gathered 'round was not one to give up on. So I decided to chase my jackpot dreams in 2015 with not only one trip to Vegas à la my husband's work conference, but also with a quick return a couple months later for my mom's fiftieth birthday.

For the first 2015 Vegas trip with Chris, I had a semi-snobby demeanor because, instead of staying at our normal suite at The Venetian or The Palazzo, we had to stay at the Vdara Hotel thanks to his company's newly signed contract. *The Vdara doesn't even have a casino! Come on people!* I spent the week feeding twenty-dollar bills into machines at other hotels, eating desserts after every meal, and mentally planning the stops I'd be making with my mom once I got back for her birthday.

July arrived and Joy, my mom, and I arrived in Las Vegas after weeks of counting down the days. We headed to The Venetian (*fine, I'll pay for a room there if I can't get one for free*) where we stayed for the next four days.

This Vegas trip was a little different for me. I was six months in on my Gals with Goals blog and my goal for the month was learning to play poker and playing in a Vegas casino. I had publicly announced and documented my story of how I was learning to play poker over the past few weeks. My grand finale for my poker experience would be playing at a real table in Vegas. So while I knew I would hit the slot machines on that trip, I was a little distracted with my poker plans.

The only thing I was concerned about as we unpacked at the hotel was grabbing dinner and figuring out when and where I was going to play my first-ever official game of poker. The thought of poker had taken over my brain. Like all good goals I'd set for myself, I wanted to back out when I saw a packed poker room full of men who looked like they hadn't moved from their seats in three days. Fear invaded my body. *Seriously, where are the women at the tables? And what if you have to go to the bathroom?*

With the time change and the fact that we didn't

want to be zombies the following days, we decided to grab dinner at the Grand Luxe Café in the lobby and gamble at The Venetian and The Palazzo for the night. That meant any one of us could just head up to the room if we were broke or tired and no one had to make their way back down The Strip in the dark by themselves.

Five minutes after being in the room and counting our cash for the hundredth time, we all crammed a few hundred bucks in our cross-body purses and headed to dinner. We anxiously awaited dinner as we gazed out into the casino and chatted about our game plans.

We *always* came to the casino with a plan. Sometimes that plan was always max betting, or only playing penny slots, or playing a specific machine we'd had luck on last time. Sometimes that plan was simply a superstitious combo of sitting on the right-hand side of an aisle, right foot propped-up, while pushing the button with our left hands. *Anything for that jackpot, people. Give me a rabbit's foot and I'm not ashamed to wave it over the machine before I insert my cash.*

On this particular night I had two game plans. First, I'd visit the poker room and observe what was happening. Even though I promised myself and all my blog readers I would be playing in a Vegas casino, I had never actually played a *real* game of poker before arriving in Vegas. I just wanted to watch others play in real-life and see if I could get the courage to try it myself over the next couple days.

The second game plan was to play a slot machine my Grandma calls "Foo Baby." I have no clue why she calls it that, but I knew she had luck on it in the past. It was a machine with little Asian characters on it, and I just-so-happened to have a little figurine that looked exactly like the characters on the machine. Chris had brought the figurine back from a business trip to Hong Kong and told me it was called the "God of Fortune." I figured between the name and the resemblance to the characters on the slot machine, *how could I not win?!*

We finished dinner and our fifteen-dollar martinis that tasted like peroxide. We toasted to my mom's birthday and the hope of winning a jackpot. I made my mom and Joy rub the head of the "God of Fortune" for good luck, and we all scooted out of the restaurant and parted ways in the casino.

On your first night in Vegas, you really have to contain yourself. It's all so exciting. You still have all your money in your pocket, you've caught a second wind despite a three-hour time difference, and every machine holds your potential new life as a millionaire. There are those initial moments when you're roaming the casino that you feel so happy and all of your life's problems fade into the background. But, on the flip side, you have to just pace yourself so you're not left with empty pockets in less than twenty-four hours on a four-day trip.

I made my way to the poker room where my suspicions were confirmed. I found that out of the hundreds of people playing the game, very few were women. I spent thirty minutes watching hundreds of men play poker while I was doing self-talk to convince myself I could hang with them in the coming days. I quickly got bored watching and headed out to the slot machines.

I sat down at a machine and put in a hundred-dollar bill. I typically never put that much into a machine at once, but what the heck—Viva Las Vegas! If it worked, it was going to be a new theory on how to win.

I won forty dollars after a few minutes and quickly lost thirty-five of it after a few more minutes. *So much for that theory.*

I cashed out and went to find "Foo Baby."

After only a few minutes I found the machine and put in my $105 ticket. Since I had only technically been gambling for about fifteen minutes, I really was far from the desperate feeling of wanting to win. I always want to win, but there's a certain focus and internal pleading with God you do when you know you're down to one hundred dollars with a day-and-a-half to go. When it's your first day gambling you're really just feeling out if you think you'll have a lucky streak this trip or not. You're not to the point of wanting to sell all your belongs on eBay just yet.

"Foo Baby," whose real name is "88 Fortunes," is a penny slot, but like all penny slots you have the option to bet multiple lines and pennies per spin. I wasn't real keen on blowing all of my money on day one, so I opted for betting on all the lines possible with a couple pennies per line, totaling $1.76 per spin.

I began daydreaming and mindlessly hitting the spin button. In a matter of a few minutes my $105 was getting closer to sixty dollars. I decided to just ride it out on that machine. I mean, I had the "God of Fortune" in my purse. Something *had* to give eventually.

I push "spin" again and I went to the bonus round. *Now we're talking!*

There are two types of bonus rounds on slot machines. There's the kind where the machine simply does what it's going to do while you sit and clap and wiggle around waiting to see your fate. Then there's the other kind where you're asked to select coins or people or characters and you have some ability to determine the outcome. I'm not a big fan of the ones where you have to choose, because if you choose the genie with the least amount of free coins behind it, you suddenly start beating yourself up for always selecting the character on the far left because you read online somewhere that it will pay the highest.

So here I was in the bonus round of "Foo Baby," and I was asked to select coins until three of them matched. Behind each coin was a "grand jackpot," "major jackpot," or "mini jackpot." I've selected these coins several times and I know how this works. You pick coins and eventually you win the mini jackpot of eleven dollars and some change. You may get the major jackpot of thirty-two dollars if you're really lucky. *It's a penny slot, what do you expect?*

I select a coin: grand jackpot.

I select another coin: grand jackpot.

I select another coin: mini jackpot.

I select another coin: grand jackpot.

GRAND JACKPOT!

I WON THE GRAND JACKPOT!

I hadn't even educated myself on what each jackpot was worth past mini and major, knowing that the odds of getting anything higher than those were slim to none.

I glanced up to the top of the machine in hopes of seeing the grand jackpot total, but the machine had reset itself, like it does when someone wins the largest possible jackpot.

All the coins and characters on my screen disappeared. The screen went black.

"Call Attendant to pay Jackpot Win $20,206.27" suddenly appeared in white font on the black screen.

Call Attendant?

Jackpot?

Win?

$20,206.27?!

There were no bells, no whistles, no Asian-inspired music playing in the background, and no crowd of people shaking me and high-fiving me. Rather, a silent machine blinked a light to signal the need for an attendant and a black screen told me I had won $20,206.27.

I became numb.

My stomach started hurting.

I got my phone out and called my mom.

My heart started beating so hard I could feel it in my arms. My hands began shaking as I waited for her to pick up. She said, "What did you do? We've only been here fifteen minutes!" She was worried because we follow two basic casino etiquette rules:

1. Only call if you win something really big. Anything under $1,000 does not qualify as "big."

2. Only call if you're broke and you're headed to the room so no one thinks you got kidnapped when they can't find you.

I stuttered as I said "Mommm . . . I *think* I just won twenty thousand dollars on a slot machine." I was so nervous that I may have been incorrectly reading the machine that I even hesitated to say the words "twenty thousand dollars."

Her tone switched to a serious one like it used to before she would punish me. "NO YOU DID NOT! Are you serious?!"

There may have been some language not suitable for children thrown in there.

I said, "Yes, my screen is black and it says an attendant is coming. I can't talk because I see them coming my way. I'm next to Wheel of Fortune outside of the poker room. Come find me." She proceeded to squeal, said additional curse words, and confirmed she was on her way.

The attendant, who ironically enough was Asian, said, "Oh, you won the big one!" while asking for my license and social security number. On any other day, I would've been hesitant to share my social security number because Chris had lectured me on identity theft, but I would've given blood and hair samples at this point to get my hands on the loot. The attendant asked if I wanted the payout in cash.

I said, "Sure! *Wait*, I'm still not convinced I even won this much. What's the other option?"

He said "check" but shrugged with a kind of, "I don't really want to have to do a check" demeanor.

I said, "Cash is fine," and he left to get my jackpot as my mom and Joy came skipping my way.

My mom was jumping, Joy was saying "OH MY GOSH," and they were both squeezing me a lot, saying "I can't even believe this, I can't even believe this." My mom was sending texts and calling friends and family members as Joy asked me how it all went down. I called Chris and told him of our newfound money. He said, "Are they going to fly me out there?" several times over. I'm not sure who "they" were, and no one on the casino staff discussed chartering a plane for him, but I was gloating with pride as I was now the wife who won a jackpot.

Think of the stories he would tell his friends! Think of how popular I would be!

My mom took my picture next to the slot machine as I worried if they would take my jackpot away for breaking some sort of picture rule. I once had a casino attendant tell me I couldn't film a slot machine when I had gone to a bonus round. I'm a rule-follower, so I've been nervous ever since that experience.

A short time later, the attendant and a lady in a suit arrived with two stacks of hundred-dollar bills wrapped in $10,000 paper wrappers, two loose hundred-dollar bills, a five-dollar bill, and a one-dollar bill. I assume they gave me the twenty-seven cents, but I have no recollection of any more cash other than the large stacks of bills. I gave the attendant a two-hundred-dollar tip because I had once seen my Grandma tip when she'd won $6,000 on a slot machine. Otherwise, I would have been oblivious to this expectation. *Note to self: get job as casino attendant and only serve those who win jackpots.*

I put the cash in the Nike purse I'd had since 2006 as Joy, my mom, and I dashed off to the hotel room to put the moolah in the safe. Since Chris was thousands of miles away packing for a fake-chartered private jet, he couldn't help me with the hotel room safe, so I did several tests before I released my cash to its new, little, safe home. We all squealed some more. I emailed my boss and coworkers to let them know I had finally won the jackpot I'd been saying I would win for years.

I felt a huge separation between me and the people who won jackpots and didn't tell anyone. *Who are those people?* Had they given me a giant check, I would've likely posed in the splits in front of it and blast-posted the photos all over social media before even depositing it. I proceeded to send private messages to every Facebook friend I had as my mom and Joy went back to the casino in hopes of having such luck themselves.

I had done it. I had won a jackpot. It wasn't a million dollars or enough to quit my job, but I had won the most you could win on that slot machine, and I had two stacks of hundred-dollar bills in a safe to prove it.

Less than twelve hours after I'd won a grand jackpot, my mind was already racing with what to do with the money. It didn't take long before I secretly thought, *Okay, now I see how the lottery ruins people's lives.*

I kept thinking of all the other people who could use the money and the guilt of why I won started creeping in.

I consoled my jackpot-winning self by buying one pair of Christian Louboutin shoes for $1,000. (Yes, they hurt my feet, and yes, I will pretend they don't for all of eternity.) I also paid for the breakfast buffet at the Flamingo for my mom and Joy where I ate ice cream and macaroni and cheese for breakfast. *I could no longer even make sensible food choices. I had too much cash to worry about.*

I exchanged emails with Chris over the next couple days with a list of options for what we could do with the money. I had divvied up some of the pot among various family members who could use a dime or two, I noted how it would pay for our upcoming vacation, and I was suggesting the rest would live in the bank until carelessness or material items we couldn't live without were advertised on Google ads (or for when taxes would come back to bite me in the ass).

He was agreeable to the plan, and we shared the money love when I returned home the following week by sending checks to a handful of family members.

I never thought I would really win a jackpot. I mean, I would get delusional sometimes and force-feed money into slot machines in the hopes of winning one, but I didn't think I would actually be carrying $20,000 around in my faded sports purse.

Other than the shoes and a subsequent vacation, the money didn't result in a new car, a new wardrobe, a home remodel, or anything else crazy people asked me if I was planning to buy.

The money ended up making me get face-to-face with my love for people. It made me dig deeply on my generosity meter and ask myself what was important to me. It made me consider how I would feel going over the deep end on material items while knowing a few hundred dollars or a $1000 of the winnings would ease a grocery bill or two for others. (The shoes don't count. I was in a fog.)

The money made me feel guilty. It made me question why things happen for some people and not others. It made me wonder if it was pure luck or if God flipped that third "grand jackpot" coin for me in hopes that I would be a catalyst for dispersing the money to those who needed it.

I always thought a jackpot would make for a good story and get me a year closer to that black Mercedes I've had my eye on. I thought that if it were big enough, I'd pay off our house and we'd become official hoarders of all things Pottery Barn. Instead, the joy of generosity felt better than the joy of heated leather seats and cable knit throw pillows.

But someday, if I win a *million* dollars . . .

CALL ME. CARRY ME. SEE ME.

"Look people in the eye when they're talking to you."

– Lisa Lovely

I AM A CHRISTIAN, BUT I wasn't raised in the church. I was there for preschool, I was there with friends, and I was there more frequently when my stepmom entered our lives. In sixth grade, I went to church with a friend and walked to the front of the youth group and accepted Jesus into my heart. I can't say I totally understood what that meant, but I felt called to go up and do it. I left with an overwhelming amount of questions when a man later caught me in the back of the room and told me the Lord wrote my name down in His book of angels who will be going to Heaven.

I proceeded to live a rule-following life, I became close with Christian friends my senior year in high school, and in college I found myself living with friends with whom I attended Campus Crusade for Christ meetings. I "accepted Jesus into my heart" or was "saved" or "claimed that Jesus Christ is my Lord and Savior" several more times throughout those years.

I am like others though. I don't attend church regularly, though I do pray every day, multiple times a day. I lean on God often, mostly daily, but I don't have many deep discussions about Him outside of the occasional women's retreat or friend of a friend's life group I may hang out with every once in a while. Also, I have no real understanding of the Bible.

Where to start in the Bible tends to not be common dinnertime talk, and honestly I am oftentimes ashamed to say I can't explain the difference between the Old and New Testaments. I am embarrassed to say I can't really quote Scripture, and if I could I oftentimes don't understand what I'm reading or saying. I have found that many biblical references I connect with come from listening to Christian music daily.

For those reasons, I tend not to share about Jesus. I don't really share how He works in my life or even open conversation about what He's doing in others' lives because I can't tie it back to the Word. There are people who have read the Bible—like, all the way through. There are people who teach the Bible weekly. Instead of asking and connecting with these people, I often nod and am like so many others whom, I'm guessing, can never actually get to the spot in the Bible the pastor is referencing until it's time for the closing prayer.

God works in mysterious ways though. He has

recently been calling me to open my Bible and to ask questions and to share my lack of knowledge in hopes of drawing others closer. So I will.

Despite my lack of Bible-quoting and Scripture-sharing gifts, there are words God has placed in my mind and soul in the last few years. These phrases enter in a timely manner and are on replay when I need to hear them most. I am going to share those words, and I am going to fearlessly tie them to Scripture. I am likely going to be incorrect in my interpretation, and I am likely going to feel self-conscious about the words I share. But I have heard it said that to be Christian is to be Christ-like. I have been called in the last year to be Christ-like through the following three commands.

"I will call you by name."

My love of people has grown over the years. I am proud to say I have matured out of a gossipy high school girl and into a woman who values people and strives to be gentle with her words about others, praise Jesus. The command "I will call you by name" has played in my mind this year in times where I'm face-to-face with someone who needs me to call them by name.

I work in downtown Columbus in an area that attracts mostly corporate workers. It's a safe area with plenty of restaurants and places to stop within walking distance. I pass the occasional homeless person on the street, but for the most part I'm surrounded with people who live a similar life to mine.

I found myself this past summer walking to a local market for lunch on a frequent basis. I was on an organic food kick, and it wasn't uncommon to spend a pretty penny for a lunch that forced something green onto my plate. But every day I would walk by the same homeless lady who held a cardboard sign asking for money. I began to feel so convicted about it. I was walking by her every day as if she weren't human. I was walking by her in my dress clothes on my way to get a fifteen-dollar lunch and a four-dollar coffee, and I couldn't even stop to acknowledge her in any human basic way.

"I will call you by name."

"I will call you by name."

I couldn't ignore this command any longer. I came home and filled a bag with personal hygiene products and food and planned to give it to her the following day. While I was giving her these material items, I had one thing in mind: to learn her name.

As I gave her the bag and she thanked me profusely, I shook her hand and introduced myself. I asked her name and she replied, "Faye." *She shares a name with my great-grandmother.* I told her when I see her around that I will be sure to call her by name.

"But now, this is what the LORD says – he who created you, Jacob, he who formed you, Israel: 'Do not fear, for I have redeemed you; I have summoned you by name; you are mine'" (Isaiah 43:1).

"I will carry you."

Life deals us some crazy cards. Life isn't fair. Life rewards one while simultaneously challenging another. Life brings joy and sorrow—sometimes it feels like *only* joy or *only* sorrow. Life leaves us asking, "Why me?" and "Why them?" on a daily basis. Life can be an uphill battle while it seems like a free ride for others.

As blessings have occurred in my life this year—relationships, finances, stability, happiness, contentment, freedom, and joy—life is handing me opportunities for others.

"I will carry you."

"I will carry you."

In times of wealth in feelings and things, there are people in our lives who need to be carried. They need our physical, emotional, and unconditional arms to carry them, literally or metaphorically. They need to know that when we're on a peak, we can reach our arms down in their valley and carry them, for as long and as tirelessly as they need.

I have been given opportunities to cook a meal for a neighbor, to listen to people's mistakes without judgment, and to provide resources when they are sparse for others. Say, "This really sucks, and I'm going to sit here with you while it sucks" with people. I will carry them until they reach their peak.

"Even to your old age and gray hairs I am he, I am he who will sustain you. I have made you and will carry you; I will sustain you and I will rescue you" (Isaiah 46:4).

———————

"I will see you."

The digital world is threatening our ability every day to see people. I have just as many electronic devices as the next person, and I am fighting the addiction like the rest of the world.

In a world full of electronic messages and social media, I hear my command:

"I will see you."

"I will see you."

I am being reminded on a daily basis: see people. I commit to looking people in the eye when they talk to me and limiting all distractions in my physical and mental surroundings. I not only see them for what they're bringing to my physical space, but I am looking into their eyes to identify what they're bringing for me to see that may not always be as easy to spot. I am being called to look at them, listen to them, and make them feel seen.

I have committed during my work day, or in interactions with friends, that I will not let an electronic device capture my attention when a person who is requesting my attention is right in front of me. All I have to do is see them eye-to-eye.

"I remain confident in this: I will see the goodness of the LORD in the land of the living" (Psalm 27:13).

Brooke Ignet Hocker

NEVER

"Never show 'em that you're smart or you'll get stuck

doing all the work."

– Lisa Lovely

Brooke Ignet Hocker

POLITICKS

"Say what you mean and mean what you say."

– Lisa Lovely

Politicks | /pa-le-tiks/ | noun: the exhaustion and shame felt during conversations related to the personal preference(s) and knowledge of candidates running for power over a city, region, or country. Symptoms are similar to that of a tick bite: hard to find initially, but commonly result in bloodsucking overreactions.

I'VE BEEN CARRYING A SECRET SINCE I was eighteen years old. This secret has become increasingly more difficult to hide as I get older and surround myself with friends from Corporate America or those who listen to podcasts for fun.

I have never voted.

I'm not even registered.

I may have registered once when I was in college while standing in line at the dining hall. It's just as likely that what I signed was a credit card application or petition for locally sourced foods in the cafeteria, *all in the name of a free pen.*

Despite the massive amount of yard signs, commercials where candidates bash each other, televised political debates, and general political chitchat in the office, I'm always unaware of when Election Day is and all of the things I'm supposed to know about voting. It's not until I'm silently shamed by the number of people wearing "I voted today" stickers that I begin to see the privilege I am dismissing. In that moment, I begin to feel embarrassed, the way you do when you volunteer at a nonprofit and leave in your luxury car.

Every time an election rolls around, whether local or presidential, I spend the entire day hoping to avoid contact with anyone who may ask if I've voted yet. I feel like an awful person, an awful woman, and an awful American. I want to hide. I want to find a way to leave work early and join society again the following day when we can all just complain about the outcomes and suddenly no one cares if you actually voted.

At 7:00 a.m. on Election Day, people with *the sticker* start discussing where they voted, what time they arrived at the polls, and how far the venue was from their home. I always envision general shenanigans that may have happened within the appropriate mileage outside of the polls. I picture college-age political science interns in semi-wrinkly, white button-up shirts, with name badges hanging on long beaded necklaces, attempting last minute campaigning for their favorite candidate, *but I've never actually been to the polls myself to witness if this is fact or fiction.*

On Election Day, the very people who can never seem to get to work on time are suddenly in line at 6:00 a.m. waiting to determine the fate of Ohio's marijuana laws or to "Say yes!" to a school levy that seems to make its appearance on the ballot every year (*as if I've ever seen a real ballot*) and threatens to cut all sports programs from local public schools if it doesn't pass.

I suddenly feel like I'm on the outside and everyone knows a secret I was supposed to know. Everyone knows about Election Day and the details around the issues that are up for debate, but no one told me. I know personal responsibility comes into play, but I always feel slighted in some way. No one was talking about voting the day before, but now everyone has cotton fuzz stuck to the back of their "I voted today" sticker. They managed to change their childcare and carpool plans around just for the occasion. It's like knowing you should back up data on your laptop or how to do your taxes. *Are we all just supposed to know? Who is teaching us this stuff?*

I can typically fight off the early morning voters and not let them in on my secret. When they ask me if I've voted yet, a simple no generally implies I'll be an evening voter. They typically close the conversation with suggestions of times to go based on their experience waiting in line that morning.

It's the late voters who make me nervous. It's the

people who leave the office at 5:00 p.m. making a mad dash to the polls. It's the people who think they can defy traffic on Election Day and start commiserating about it with the rest of us on the elevator. It's the people who start gathering stats in the elevator on who did or didn't vote already. It's the people who proceed to ask detailed questions about the location and standard wait times everyone experienced while voting.

I don't even know how to answer when these people ask me if I've voted yet. I don't have the sticker and I'm not leaving work in a rush. *Clearly, I'm the worst representation of a female American with the right and privilege to influence this city, state, and country's future direction. And now they're going to make me say it.* They're going to not only make me say that I haven't voted, but they're going to make me say I've never voted when they ask me where I've voted in the past.

Why is everyone so interested in poll locations?!

And when did everybody get into wearing stickers?!

I begin praying that anyone, regardless of political parties, morals, or even general conversation-interruption skills, will bail me out. I pray that someone jumps in as we all stand shoulder-to-shoulder in the elevator to say something about how they heard that a certain location had shorter lines in the evening. If I'm lucky, they'll throw in something about expected traffic length and their thoughts on gay marriage, *which will hopefully deflect the shame I'm feeling until we reach the lobby.*

Politics wasn't something my family and I really

discussed growing up. We didn't discuss recent laws that were passed or issues that were teed up for upcoming elections. We're a family who would rather discuss "What would you do if you won a million dollars?" over Thanksgiving dinner than one that debates our political points of view while hammering our favorite candidate's marketing materials into our yard.

While they do vote, I honestly can't tell you if my parents are Republicans or Democrats. I have always been okay with that. It always sounded miserable when I heard friends talk about how their parents argued with their aunts and uncles for hours after dinner on who should be the front-runner in the primaries.

As of a few years ago, I couldn't have even articulated the difference between a Republican and a Democrat. Even now, the way I would describe each is based on my perception of both parties as a result of what I see on social media and observing the people in my life who are outspoken about their political affiliations (*also known as the people I try to avoid having dinner with on a regular basis*). And while many sport *the sticker* on Election Day and I begin to feel less-than for not casting a vote, I do wonder how well others would describe both parties.

Republican | \ri-ˈpə-bli-kən\ | noun: Corporate, suits, savers and retirement-fund builders, investors, believers in the Bible, prone to posting derogatory cartoons about Democrats, political bumper stickers on SUVs, gun owners, middle- to upper-class white men, pro-life and prone to picketing, on school boards, or boards of any kind, inclined to say how their tax dollars are going toward people who didn't work for it.

Democrat | \ˈde-mə-ˌkrat\ | noun: Free spirits, lovers of the arts, focused more on humanitarian work and less on dollars, pro-choice, supporters of gay pride, commonly found saying, "Let's bring our boys home" when referring to deployed soldiers, likely to have attended Woodstock-type events, focused on people and communities, recyclers, likely to have spent a year in nonprofit or service positions.

―――――――

I remember a presidential election going on when I was in elementary school. I know this because our teacher asked everyone to write down who they would vote for. I'm not sure if this was supposed to be a lesson in government or just a way for our teacher to see how our parents were voting, but I remember everyone in the class saying they were going to write down George Bush's name.

Along with one other student, I wrote down "Ross Perot." I never thought Ross Perot would win. I didn't even know who Ross Perot was. I just knew he wouldn't get a lot of votes and I felt bad for him, so I voted for him in our fake election.

I guess that means I'm an Independent?

Once I resigned as Ross Perot's local elementary school campaign manager, politics only resurfaced in my life during high school when Bill Clinton got caught with his pants down in the Oval Office and Monica Lewinsky became a household name. I became intrigued by the pseudo-documentary specials they would run on TV about the scandal. The videos typically showed Bill Clinton making public appearances and shaking Monica Lewinsky's hand while doing some sort of super-secret lingo that body language experts cracked the code on: *A glance to the left meant he wanted to meet up with her later. Scratching his face on the right meant he couldn't talk to her right then.* Who knows what Bill Clinton's platform and beliefs were, but we all knew Monica Lewinsky put the blue dress on the map for the official uniform of the president's mistress.

No one talked about politics in college. I don't recall my friends voting, and I never saw an "I voted today" sticker during those years.

During post-college-move-out-get-a-real-job phase, *Saturday Night Live* was knocking it out of the park with their political skits. I would never watch the show, but I did a lot of fake laughing when my friends would do reenactments of their favorite lines. How did they know what these jokes meant? *How do they stay up so late? What will they say if I ask what this stuff means?*

At this point, I was too far gone to ask questions. I felt stupid asking people about candidates or what it means to be a Republican or a Democrat, so I just worked from home to avoid traffic every few years when presidential candidates were speaking downtown near my work and suppressed the shame by finding any channel on TV that wasn't talking politics (*Thank you, Bravo*).

Once I was a full-blown adult, with a husband and everything, it was time for another presidential election. All signs pointed to Barack Obama becoming the next President of the United States. My interest was piqued toward the tail end of the election, and I found myself pulling for him to win.

I guess that means I'm a Democrat?

I began to make an effort to learn about what he stood for, and I felt more engaged than any other election simply because I knew "Yes We Can" was his campaign slogan. I found some inspiration in all of it despite the large distance between me and the polls. As I watched TV reporters announce that Barack Obama had officially won, I felt completely embarrassed and ashamed that I had not taken any responsibility to learn more—or participate as a voter.

———

I'm not proud that I've never voted. I'm ashamed that I haven't taken responsibility to learn about issues my community and my country are facing. I cringe that I have close friends who have gone overseas to fight for our country while I have not even educated myself enough to do what I can to help too. I'm embarrassed every time I get my driver's license renewed and I say no when they ask if I'm a registered voter.

I will vote in the next election.

I will get my sticker.

I invite everyone hiding the same secret to join me.

Who wouldn't want the ballot to read "Donald Trump vs. Hillary Clinton" during their first trip to the polls?

ONLY CHILD SYNDROME

"There's a difference between being spoiled and being a

spoiled brat." – Lisa Lovely

I AM AN ONLY CHILD. WELL, technically I'm not, but for the majority of my life I was living my life sans siblings. Shortly before my seventeenth birthday, my dad and stepmom had a baby whom I now call my sister, and ten years later I picked up a couple stepsisters along the way on my mom's side. But for all standard definitions of how one was raised, I was an only child.

Being an only child is the only thing I've known of childhood and my place in our family, but I realized in a recent conversation with a friend how the life of an only child feels like a mystery to most. It's like a secret life for those who grew up as the oldest, the middle, or the youngest. When my friend realized her son would likely be an only child, she had a long list of questions for me about my experience and feelings on the situation.

For my dear friends who are the oldest of a small army of children, for the friends who are sandwiched between an older beautiful sister who could be a model and a baby sister with a Ph.D., for those of you who received all the hand-me-downs and have only ever owned items that belonged to your three older brothers first, and for those who wed a partner who is an "only," let me dispel the myths and shine a light on the facts of life as an only.

———

Myth: Onlys are sad.

Only children aren't sad, at least no more so than your average thirteen-year-old with braces and bangs that are long overdue for a haircut. Contrary to popular belief, only children do not spend their time pondering what life would be like with a sibling. They don't even know that that's something they should (or shouldn't) be thinking about. The majority of only children do not beg their parents to give them a sibling while staring longingly at a family of six at a restaurant.

———

Fact: Onlys are more mature than your average kid.

Unless they have an entourage of cousins whom they're close with, an only child's standard days, nights, and weekends are spent with a primarily adult crowd. There's no "kids table" at their dinners, no cartoon marathons all weekend, and no child-themed bedrooms. Typically, the child is fitting into the adult life their parents have already established. They are joining conversations the adults are having. They are expected and told to "act like an adult" even at age six. They sit at grown-up tables with grown-up utensils and speak complete grown-up sentences earlier than other kids their age.

———————

Fact: Onlys value privacy.

Only children don't have to share space and things with siblings, so even a shared space in their later years can feel like an invasion of their life and secrets. As adults, only children may come across with a harsh "DON'T TOUCH MY STUFF" tone, but it's really that they just don't want someone else's slimy little hands wrapped around their box of journals they've been keeping since third grade. They don't really have secrets to hide per se, but they're aware of the value of certain items and need a place to call those things their own. (See also: don't rummage through their things when they're not around, and give them time to themselves).

———————

Myth (though sometimes fact): Onlys are bad at sharing.

Just because an only child doesn't have a sibling to share material items with doesn't necessarily mean they're bad at sharing. If they have even halfway decent parents who have taught them respect, they can share a board game or their favorite stuffed animal if forced. They are also better equipped to share their feelings as they are used to being the center of conversation or questions and are prepared to respond quickly and appropriately.

On the contrary, while only children have the ability to share, they do not enjoy or find value in sharing meals. They will not order one dessert and ask for two spoons. They loathe a group decision on the best appetizers to order for a group of coworkers. They would rather pay for the entire table to get their own dinner or dessert instead of having to cut a chicken breast or steak in half, or watch their social circle grab fries off their plate. While becoming college roommates with an only child or sharing deep dark secrets with them are encouraged, please do not plan for family-style entrees at group lunches or double-date dinners.

Myth: Onlys do not like going to their spouse's large family parties.

As adults, only children don't dislike going to their spouse's large family gatherings, but they need a few minutes to adjust when they arrive. Things at an only child's house are quiet, organized, and normally include more intimate discussions around a small table. More personal information is shared, and everyone knows what is going on in everyone's life.

Once they arrive at their spouse's large family

gatherings, they will need a few minutes to adjust to the fact that a door was left open, there's something spilled on a kitchen counter that no one is cleaning up, a group of cousins just started at movie at 11:00 p.m. in the other room, and there's a toddler eating things off the floor whom no one is watching. Adult onlys may appear uptight in these situations, but know it's because they crave connection and conversation—and they're worried about the toddler. Give them space and they will have the ability to join the fun.

———————

Fact: Onlys have a strong sense of loyalty to their parents.

Only children know they are their parent's only child, and for that they build an extreme sense of loyalty. They learn at a very early age the importance of their presence, participation, and enthusiasm for all holidays, events, accomplishments, and celebrations. Therefore, the bond with their parents is deeply rooted and is on a continuum through adulthood. Onlys are also more likely to regularly call home for as long as there's a home to call.

———————

Myth: Onlys are lonely.

Only children grow up to become the type of people who go to restaurants and movies by themselves—by choice. This isn't a reflection that they're sad, lonely, or depressed; this is simply the way they recharge. Even an extroverted only child can be found seeking out opportunities for a breakfast or dinner out at a restaurant by themselves. They are comfortable doing this and even crave it at times. Do not invite yourself to their plans. Do not accompany them to bathroom trips. Let them fly solo when they so desire.

Myth: Onlys are spoiled brats.

Any child, with or without siblings, ultimately has the potential to act in a way that leaves a babysitter calling them a brat behind their back when they leave. If a child (whether an only, oldest, middle, or youngest) has parents who taught them how to function in this world without carrying a selfish and entitled demeanor, then that child won't be a brat.

Now, only children are positioned to have the highest risk of becoming brats simply due to their potential to receive a higher number of material items compared to their friends with a house full of siblings. However, such spoiling is often offset by the amount of intentional parenting and guidance an only child's parents can give them because there's only one of them. Just because a child is spoiled does not mean they're groomed to become a brat.

Fact: Onlys need extra words of affirmation.

If you're married to an only child, tell them

they're amazing all of the time. Discover what you love about them and be relentless in your desire to tell them. You are the new replacement for a set of parents who have been doing this for them since birth.

Every day. Tell them every day.

Brooke Ignet Hocker

PMS

"Women who are in prison for murder all had PMS when

they committed their crimes." – Lisa Lovely

"Premenstrual Syndrome: a powerful spell that women are put under about once every month, which gives them the strength of an ox, the stability of a Window's OS, and the scream of a banshee. Basically man's worst nightmare." – urbandictionary.com

———————

Dear Former Stepdad,

I wouldn't say the fact that my mom called you a f*#k*ng idiot was really her fault at all, and hopefully this didn't play a major role in you guys getting divorced. When she said that, you see, she was just mad you hadn't toasted the bread on the BLT she

69

asked you to make for her. She'd been craving a BLT for a week, which we were all aware of, so when you simply put bacon, lettuce, and tomato between two pieces of white bread that didn't even have so much as a slight tan to them, it was kind of your own fault. Anyone would've reacted that way. Same goes for when she cried about the way you added fabric softener to the clothes in the washer. You did this to yourself.

Sincerely,
Your Former Stepdaughter

————

Dear Girl in the Elevator,

I don't want to sigh loudly and walk on your heels, but it's your own fault for walking too slowly all the time. I try to be patient with you, but that only lasts approximately twenty-one days. This isn't my fault that I'm appearing rude. This is your fault for walking too slowly all the time.

Sincerely,
Move

————

Dear All My Girlfriends,

It's probably better you don't even know we're fighting right now. I realize we haven't talked in a month or two, and there isn't anything specifically to be mad at you for, but you know what you did. Everything is your fault and will be until next week. And stop with the Facebook selfies.

Sincerely,
Your Frenemy

———

Dear Husband,

Must you make noise when you walk around or do things?! EVERYTHING IS YOUR FAULT!

Love,
Your Wife

———

Dear Guy with the Chips,

Stop chewing chips right now or I will kill you and dump crumbled chips on your body and I won't feel bad for one second.

Love,
Sound Sensitive

———

Dear Everyone Before 9:00 a.m.,

Stop talking to me. I see all of you often and have always disliked things about you, but really, it's your fault that I'm being mean to you this week. You're stupid, ugly, and dumb. That is not my problem. Your hair looks dumb too. I've always thought that. These are real feelings. And totally rational.

Sincerely,
Cool, Calm, and Collected

———

Dear CVS,

It's cute that you do paired marketing and put the Snickers bar display right next to the Tampon aisle. I see what you're doing and I raise a glass to you!

Sincerely,
Stop Looking in My Cart

532 CLYDE LLC

"The only thing worse than cleaning up your own filth is

cleaning up somebody else's." – Lisa Lovely

L IKE MOST TWENTY-TWO-YEAR-OLDS coming out of four years at a large university with a bachelor's degree in the social sciences, I graduated on the hottest day of the year with one hundred dollars in my checking account and no "real job" in sight. My options were limited, especially since I offered my well-educated psychological counsel to friends and family for free. When my friends said, "You're really good at giving advice," I found that didn't actually translate to a real job or a salary. After an hour of family photos and packing up my final belongings from my college apartment, I headed back home to start the process of becoming an adult. I debated if I should still shop for suits in the juniors department at Kohl's.

I had planned to move back in with my mom and follow the savings schedule she'd created for me. The plan included living at home for one year, saving the majority of my paychecks, and then buying my first house. My parents told me how much it would pay off in the long run to buy versus rent. I already felt more mature at the thought of it all. I told everyone who gave me grief for moving back home that I was going to be purchasing a house soon.

After I bought a suit. And found a job.

On the two-month anniversary of my college graduation, which also doubled as the deadline my mom had imposed before I had to "just take any job," I received an offer for my first grown-up salaried position. I dodged the bullet on having to go back to being a cashier at the local grocery store or working in the factory that I had worked in for the last four summers.

I had a $26,000 per year salary, benefits, and a shitty schedule.

I was an adult!

My mom advised me to save $500 per paycheck over the next year to be used for a down payment on a house. I followed the plan as she instructed and frequently looked ahead on the spreadsheet she created, imagining what it would be like to actually have $10,000 in the bank. I wore cheap suits and worked through lunch breaks while my friends moved to more luxurious cities like Columbus, New York, and Atlanta and took 100 percent commission-based jobs.

When my family seeks goals, we tend to pull the trigger when we're about 50 to 60 percent through our original plan. I had planned to save $10,000 and then find the house of my $26,000 per year dreams. That was, until my Grandma just so happened to find a potential house for me when my account balance held $5,500.

My Grandma is the owner of fifteen or so properties around Dayton, Ohio and Lexington, Kentucky, all of which she rents to a cast of characters who have kept her chasing rent payments for thirty years. She is always in-the-know about what's on the market and keeps an eye out for the latest deals as she flips through the Sunday Real Estate section of the newspaper every week. She spent a number of years working at a carpet store and often invited into people's personal lives as they bought carpet for new homes or properties that were about to go on the market.

As luck would have it, my Grandma had just helped a ninety-two-year-old lady looking to buy carpet for her home which she was about to list for sale. Frances's eyes were piercing blue. Through my Grandma's calm and approachable nature, she convinced blue-eyed Frances to let her see the house before Frances listed it with a realtor. My Grandma asked Frances to hold off on buying carpet until she had a chance to check out the scene.

A week later, my Grandma was giving me a tour of Frances's 972 square foot, three-bedroom, brick ranch house with 1950s green and black tile throughout, some of which was covered with large pieces of shag carpet. It smelled like the basement of my best friend's church. My Grandma told me how much potential the house had and how great a deal it would be if I made an offer before Frances listed it with a realtor. I wasn't in love with the color of the brick on the outside, but for a twenty-two-year-old single girl with $5,500 to her name, I had to make trade-offs somewhere.

My dad accompanied me to all of my home loan meetings, and a couple days later I received a fax (yes, fax) from the office stating I was pre-approved for an $85,000 loan. *The world was mine.* I was already priding myself on the moment I would tell my renting friends about my new purchase.

I bought the house for $75,000. I was officially the owner of 532 Clyde Place.

Frances left me two wine glasses on a shelf in the kitchen with a congratulatory note.

My mom told me I was living the American dream. *I believed her.*

I painted every room in the house. I bought brand new white carpet. I furnished it with hand-me-down furniture. I did a poor job mowing the lawn every other week. I hid in my bedroom when it would get dark out, and I managed to only have to call my dad about a strange noise outside one time in three years. The house was great and often the center of conversation when my parents bragged about me to their friends.

After three years of making the house my home, the recession of 2007 was hiding around the corner. I was working in real estate advertising at the time and saw my income tank as a result of realtors not having the marketing budgets they once did.

I was a couple years into a serious relationship and dropped hints of wanting to get married into every conversation I could. My boyfriend had already moved to Columbus for a new job, and I knew life would end up taking me there too if we ever got married.

In preparation for the married life I wanted, I listed the house for sale.

A "FOR SALE" sign went up in the spring. The summer came and went and the sign remained in the lawn that was always two days overdue for a trim. Trick-or-treaters walked around the sign as they asked for candy in the fall. Snow covered the sign in the winter. By December, I had an engagement ring—but not a single offer on the house.

I'd tried every trick in the book to get the house sold. I had buried a St. Joseph figurine in the yard even though I wasn't Catholic. I had planted fake flowers in the flower box to make it look more spring-like. I had purposely left my bed unmade before work because that seemed to almost always guarantee a mid-day house showing.

As I was in the final months of wedding preparation, my fiancé and I reluctantly made the decision to rent the house for a year with plans to list it for sale again in the future. I didn't want to be a landlord but felt somewhat comforted by the fact that my Grandma was the queen of rentals and lived nearby. So I spent thirty-five dollars for a four-line ad in the newspaper:

FOR RENT: 3 bdrm, 1 bath
brick ranch. Close to school.
No smoking. No pets.
$695 deposit, $695/mo.

I put my Grandma's phone number at the end of the ad. I was mature enough to own the home but in no way mature enough to screen renters. We pretended like I put her number because I was busy at work all day and she had more free time to take calls, but I was really just suddenly afraid to talk to people and felt nervous at the thought of someone older than me wanting to rent from me. *I have always been uncomfortable and apologetic about having any level of success greater than someone who is older than me. How would I possibly handle renting to someone who was my parent's age?*

Renter #1

It only took one week to find our first renter, a single girl who was my age with twin boys in elementary school. It was one of many times I felt a maturity separation between myself and people my age with kids.

She was set to move into my house the month before my wedding, which seemed like perfect timing. I had just secured a job in Columbus that I had been commuting to and quickly ditched my "let's not live together before we're married" rule by justifying that it was only forty-five days before our big day. *I was trading my values for a $695 deposit and a year-long Band-Aid.*

I received the deposit and the first month's rent. I turned the key over to the new tenant as I packed my Honda with my last box of sweaters and journals from the house. It was frustrating and weird and sad to move into my fiancé's one-bedroom apartment while I watched another family move into my three-bedroom house, but I was too distracted by my upcoming wedding and new job to dwell on it for long. I prided myself on helping out a single mother as if I were now the reason she would make it in this world. I began paying a monthly fee for my new storage unit.

The rent checks came on time every month, and my fiancé-turned-husband and I would often say phrases like, "This renting thing isn't too bad. Maybe we should think about getting additional rental properties." We watched way too many TV shows on DIY and HGTV about house-flipping and renting during that time. Our new life as landlords seemed like a dream.

Several months into our landlord gig, I received my first phone call about a problem in the home. The soap dish in the shower had broken off, which was not surprising considering the shower wasn't one of the selling points of the house. I frantically called my Grandma and started talking fast and sweating while I asked for her opinion on what to do about it. I was scrambling for a fix and trying to prove to the renter (and myself) that I was a good landlord. I started to wonder if the renter would leave if I didn't get it fixed within twenty-four hours. My heart was beating fast and being a landlord didn't feel as easy anymore.

My Grandma sent someone over to fix the soap dish a couple days later. Every time my cell phone rang from an unknown number for the next few months, I panicked and worried if it was something more than a soap dish that needed fixing.

My sulking about living in a one-bedroom apartment subsided when my husband and I purchased a "big house," a 2,500 square foot, four-bedroom home in Columbus. We knew it was a little risky because we still owned 532 Clyde, but we had saved enough money that we would be safe should five soap dishes in the house fall off. *The American dream was no longer owning one house; it was owning two.*

A couple months later, we cashed in a gift certificate of sorts from my in-laws that covered the cost of meeting with an attorney to create a will. *Two homes and a will. I had never felt so responsible in my life.* We met with an attorney as soon as possible and talked through all the things you talk through when you create a will. After making every mature decision related to beneficiaries and medical scenarios, the attorney recommended we set up an LLC for our rental property. She told us that should a renter sue us, they could technically have rights to our "big house" too. By setting up an LLC, the only property that would be at stake would be 532 Clyde. Our "big house" still smelled like new construction. We were willing to set up ten LLCs if that's what it took to protect our home.

We left the office with a giant yellow folder full of documents and only had to wait a week before the uniquely named "532 Clyde LLC" was official. All we had to do was set up a bank account under the same name and we were more than landlords, we were business owners.

We were real grown-ups.

I contacted our renter and told her to make all checks payable to 532 Clyde LLC in the future. She made the change as instructed. Six months later she mailed a thirty-day notice informing us she would be moving to a cheaper place.

We listed the house for sale again.

Renter #2

After six months of paying for two houses while 532 Clyde was for sale, we went back to renting. I reposted the rental ad in the newspaper and had a renter lined up in no time. I still used my Grandma's phone number in the ad and blamed it on the fact that I now lived an hour-and-a-half away.

The second renter was a couple without kids. They were around my age and had been married, were then divorced, but were also attempting to reconcile. Thanks to the Fair Housing Laws, you can't be too picky when selecting a renter. While it wasn't called out explicitly in the Fair Housing documentation, I doubt choosing not to rent to a couple because I didn't think their relationship would last the term of the lease would hold up well in court.

I believe the girl had a job at a daycare center and the guy was retired or discharged from the military due to an injury. I didn't really know what all of that meant other than he had steady pay from the military, so I knew the bills would be covered.

Two days after they moved in, they called to let me know the bathtub wouldn't drain. I thought the broken soap dish from Renter #1 seemed stressful, but now I had new renters with a tub full of dirty water. I was familiar with the tub issues from when I lived there, and I already had a profile in the database at Roto-Rooter. But it all became so much more dramatic when I wasn't living there and someone else was calling for help.

I called Roto-Rooter and they were on the scene

within a couple hours. I paid via credit card over the phone. The renters were patient with me and took it all in stride. I decided I loved them and prayed they would remarry each other and stay in the house forever *despite the ugly lawn ornaments they'd put out front.*

Months went by and they paid on time—until they didn't.

They called me often to say they were breaking up again and they couldn't afford the house if only one of them lived in it. Sometimes checks came just from him, sometimes checks came from their joint account, and sometimes he would call and say the payments would be a little late.

I was patient with them because they seemed to be taking care of the house, and I even offered to reduce the rent if the girl stayed in the house alone. I cared less about sticking it to them on the terms of our rental agreement and more about just keeping the peace and avoiding the process of looking for another renter.

They broke up and moved out before the lease was up. I kept their deposit.

We listed the house for sale—again.

Renter #3

We had just watched another contract with a realtor expire with no offers when I revived my "FOR RENT" ad. I placed the ad in the newspaper and on Craigslist. This was during Craigslist's rise in popularity when everyone was buying bikes, bedframes, and buffet tables they didn't need, and just before the 2011 TV movie "The Craigslist Killer" was released and we had to start worrying about being murdered if we tried to sell the end tables in our basement. I used my Grandma's phone number in the ad again and blamed it on the fact that I had told the newspaper to just re-run the ad they had on file.

It took about six weeks before we found Renter #3, a Craigslist ad respondent. She was around my age and a single mom with five kids. While my Grandma gave me the renter's backstory, I imagined what life at my age would be like with five kids.

I never found out what she did for work, but I did know she was a student somewhere. I made up stories in my mind about how ambitious of a person she was and justified the situation to my husband and family members when we found out she would be paying her rent from some sort of government assistance. I didn't really care why she was getting assistance, but I knew that meant she would likely pay her rent on time and she was at least receiving money in some fashion for her five kids. Again, I prided myself on helping someone in need, or at least that's how I tried to look at it when I knew there was probably more to her story and a reason to be suspicious.

The first few months they lived in the house were great. I never heard a peep from them and received the rent on time every month. Spring came and my husband and I were so thankful to have a solid renter that we even went to Wal-Mart and purchased five Easter baskets for her kids as a surprise and a thank you. They weren't home when we went to drop the baskets off so we left them in the shed. We seemed to have both silently agreed to ignore the red flags that were in front of our faces when we saw the amount of junk she had piled in that shed.

A couple months later I received a letter from the city letting me know that the grass had exceeded an acceptable height. First a broken soap dish, then a tub that wouldn't drain, and now I had grass so high the city had to send a letter. I was shaking when I read the letter and felt helpless since this was something the renter had simply been too lazy or incapable of taking care of herself. I did what any mature adult would do: I called my Grandma and my parents. The grass situation suddenly became the entire family's problem.

After a phone call with the renter and a promise that she would get it taken care of that weekend, I officially hated life as a landlord and rolled my eyes at the thought that we had ever entertained the idea of acquiring more rental properties.

The weekend following the letter came quickly, and my mom did a drive-by to make sure the renter did in fact mow the jungle of a lawn. My mom called to let me know that it had not been cut but my stepdad would take care of it. He had to begin with a weed whacker because the grass was up to his thighs. I hated every minute of having to deal with it and felt guilty for having to send family members over all the time. I often imagined the neighbors, who were all retired and made their lawn maintenance a top priority, gathering together to sign a petition to have me thrown in jail over two-feet-tall grass. *I have a tendency to go to extremes in my mind when under stress, so jail seemed like the next step for my life in those moments.*

As the grass saga concluded, I received a private message on Facebook from a neighbor on Clyde. My stomach had that horrible feeling you get when you see the first few words of an email and just know the rest can't be good. She was unsure if I was still the owner of the home since the auditor's website now showed 532 Clyde LLC as the owner, but she wanted to inform me of what had recently been going on with my house and renter.

She skipped any mention of the lawn and went straight to the worst part. She told me that the renter let her kids roam the street for long hours while unsupervised (*What could I do about that?*), but more importantly, and most disgustingly, it was rumored that she had bedbugs.

I wanted to scream. I cried instead.

Bedbugs had been back on the rise and all over news stories then. The media tried to paint a picture that even the wealthiest of people could get bedbugs simply by staying at a hotel that had them hiding in all the places you would touch or set your suitcase. They said it wasn't a reflection of how clean or dirty someone's house was, but rather a problem that was extremely hard to control and easy to get if you had even set your purse down at work and someone else brought bedbugs in on their bag.

Let's get real: bedbugs are disgusting and only gross people get them.

The neighbor went on to tell me how they—the whole neighborhood was involved now—came to the conclusion that she had bedbugs due to the amount of furniture she was throwing out on the curb. Their hypothesis was also supported by the multiple visits they'd witnessed from a van with Orkin printed on the side.

I had never hoped someone was dating a man who worked for Orkin more. Maybe this was all just a bad string of rumors.

I didn't have much experience calling someone and asking if they had bedbugs, so I spent a lot of time stalling and putting down the neighbors instead. I did an amazing job of calling multiple family members to see if they'd agree with me that the neighbors were too nosy.

After a day of too much complaining, I finally had to call the renter to crack the case of the bedbug accusations. I was itchy just thinking about it. I wondered if I was going to have to burn that house down by the end of it. I ended up calling and telling her some lame story about how people had reached out to me because they were concerned about bedbugs in the neighborhood, which *technically* was true. She defensively told me how there was no way she had bedbugs and was not sure where that information was coming from. I told her I'd send my Grandma over to check things out and would pay for a company to come out and do an assessment just to be safe.

Suddenly I was the defensive one.

I never knew why I was always walking on eggshells around my renters, but I was never comfortable as a landlord and so desperately just wanted them to take care of my house. I'd even get delusional and think they'd wake up and offer to purchase it one day.

A couple days later my Grandma went to the scene. One of the renter's sons told my Grandma how his back had bites all over it and he had to get rid of his bed. My Grandma used the phrase "from the mouths of babes" when she called me. *I had never considered what that phrase meant before but I knew I hated it now*. The renter still denied having bedbugs. My Grandma confirmed that she didn't have any furniture left in the house.

I called Orkin and asked them to come out and assess the situation. They already had the address on file. The customer service rep said, "I know that house. There's bedbugs there for sure." I wanted to puke but immediately started brainstorming how I was going to keep this a secret from all the people in my life.

One hundred and thirty dollars later, Orkin called me back to say they hadn't seen bedbugs in the house but would recommend a general treatment of the home, inside and out. I wanted to do a celebratory dance, but I called another company to confirm the little devils weren't just hiding. A second pest control company assessed the situation and said there may have been bedbugs at one time, but they no longer saw any in the house. A third company confirmed they didn't see bedbugs either, and they were the lucky ones I paid to perform an inside and outside treatment *just to be safe*.

Despite the fact that I had been giving frequent updates to the neighbor who originally sent me a note through Facebook, I was sure the three additional visits from pest control companies were not building a strong case for proving bedbugs hadn't existed in the house.

The bedbug scare was my last straw with this renter. I needed her to move out even though she had continued paying me on time every month. I decided to tell her that I would be listing the house for sale and gave her more than enough time to move out. To make myself feel better, I looked up her name in the city's online public records. She had been evicted from a couple other places and had more than one run-in with the cops while driving her children around without car seats. I went back and forth between being confident in my decision to kick her out and being mad at myself for not doing a background check before she had moved in.

I had already told her that she would not be getting her deposit back given the amount of money I'd had to spend for pest control and the issues with the grass, but I ended up giving the majority of it back to her when she claimed it was the only way she could put a deposit down on a new place. I was embarrassed to tell my family I'd given her the money, but I kept trying to convince them that I was just keeping the peace so she didn't ruin anything in the house that could cost me more in the long run.

The day she finally moved out I called all of the local utility offices to get the bills changed back into my name. As the landlord curse would have it, she was amazing at paying her rent but horrible at paying her water bill. She left me with $350 in past-due water bills and a buckled wood floor in the kitchen from water that had apparently run underneath the panels (which I could never figure out how that was even possible).

The following weekend my husband and I headed back to the house. We were so tired of being landlords that we said phrases like, "I will take any offer for the house right now, even if we have to take a loss," and, "Let's just list it at a low price. I'm so sick of this." When we arrived at the house this time, my entire family was there to help clean it up and get it ready to sell, which made me cry because I was thankful for the support and because I was embarrassed it had come to that point.

We tore out carpet, painted walls, wore clothes we would rather burn than wear again, power-washed the driveway, and tried to convince ourselves that it would all turn out great.

The house didn't have a laundry room so the washer and dryer sat in the kitchen. Halfway through the cleaning fest, my husband walked out of the kitchen wearing a facemask and rubber gloves while holding a sloppy joe sandwich that had one single bite taken out of it. The sandwich had been thrown behind the dryer where it had lived for an unknown amount of time. We had reached a point of such exhaustion that there was nothing else to do other than laugh. I had shed so many tears and felt so embarrassed about the situation, all I could do was laugh so hard I almost peed my paint-stained pants and vowed to never eat a sloppy joe—or be a landlord—again.

We spent the next few weeks installing new versions of everything we had ripped out and cleaning every little bit of filth that family had left behind. I learned a lot about humility. I learned what a marijuana roach looked like too, thanks to the one they'd left in the bedroom closet.

We listed the house for sale and anxiously awaited a buyer.

During an open house weekend, someone flushed the toilet and the little lever failed to do its little-lever job so the water failed to stop running. The city called several days later to ask why we had used enough water at the house to fill an Olympic-sized pool.

We received a $900 water bill.

Renter #4

The house didn't sell and the realtor lost his real estate license due to mortgage fraud.

The new renters came as a referral. They were the daughter, boyfriend, and kids of a couple who worked with my mom. I figured a referral had to bring some peace to the situation compared to what Craigslist had delivered.

I should've known money would be an issue when the check we received for the deposit came from the renter's mother. I justified it by saying it was probably a gift to them for moving into a new house, similar to the rug my mom had bought us for our dining room when we purchased our house in Columbus.

It didn't take too long before the rent checks were either late or non-existent. I kept telling my husband that after our experience with the last renter I would trade someone not paying rent over someone not taking care of the house. I knew we had the money to cover both houses, but I didn't have the energy to deal with overgrown grass and bedbug scares again.

I used email as my primary method of communicating with the guy who was living there. Despite three previous go-rounds with renters, I still never felt mature enough to own a house that I rented out for others to live in. I always felt like a twelve-year-old, even when I knew I had the upper hand.

My renters and I developed a routine: around the first of the month I would email and ask when we could expect the rent. Sometimes I would give them until the true deadline of the fifth, but I was always disappointed that I had to contact them first. I wondered if they just thought I would ignore the fact that they weren't paying their rent.

When I was finally successful in getting money from them, it wasn't uncommon to get partial payment in cash sent through snail mail in an envelope that had been sealed with a SpongeBob SquarePants sticker. It was evident they didn't have their own checking account, but couldn't they at least put the cash in an envelope you couldn't see through and maybe leave off the cartoon sticker?

Even SpongeBob SquarePants was mocking me and my inability to take control of the situation.

As summer approached, the renters experienced the worst part about the house (excluding potential bedbugs): its lack of air conditioning. I had provided window air conditioner units, all of which were brand new with every renter as the ones before always stole them, but the house would still get pretty toasty in certain rooms. As the temperature increased, they continued to call and ask if I could install central air. I always answered by saying I would look into it, but I was always baffled by the fact that they could continue to ask me when they never paid their rent on time, if at all.

After what felt like a lifetime of chasing their rent, I received a phone call from the guy letting me know that they were breaking up and he would like me to kick her out of the house. He told me how she was doing drugs in the house and had kicked a door in during one of their fights. I started shaking when he said the word "drugs" and broke out in a pink rash when I heard about the door.

I called my mom and asked her what do. I still couldn't make it on my own when it came to being firm with people. She told me exactly what to say and do.

After leaving several voicemails for the renters, I finally got in contact with the girl. After she said, "Hello," and I said, "This is Brooke, your landlord," she instantly yelled, "YOU CAN'T KICK ME OUT!" She paused, then added, "Can you?"

My face was on fire. I shook like someone who was about to face their biggest fear. I found myself yelling at her because it was the only way she would listen. I started saying phrases my mom had told me to say: "We can either do this the easy way or the hard way. You can either move out by the end of the month, which is more than the amount of time I should give you, or I will formally evict you and you'll ruin your chances of ever finding another place to rent."

She continued to yell at me and tell me how all the things her boyfriend told me were untrue. All I could do was continue to repeat the phrases my mom instructed me to say. After several minutes of shouting at each other, she reluctantly agreed that they would move out by the end of the month while I unconvincingly threatened them about making sure the house looked like it did before they had moved in.

It was not in the same condition when they left as when they had entered.

They left me with nearly 972 square feet of furniture on the curb. My dad arranged for a dump truck to haul that away, and I added another company I had to pay over the phone. Cobweb-covered potato chips sat on top of the cabinets. Past-due electric bills resulted in dark rooms on the first day we went back to clean the place up. Broken pieces of wood laid next to the door she supposedly didn't kick in.

We listed the house for sale with a friend who was a new realtor. He had never sold a home before.

———————

The Buyer

The price of the home was now less than what I'd paid. I was disappointed at the thought of taking a loss on the home, but I had calculated the lowest amount at which we could afford to sell. In fact, I did that calculation more times than I'd ever figured out the lowest grade I could get on a final exam in order to keep a passing grade. In all the times we had the house listed in the past, we had never received a single offer. Confidence was low when it came to dreams of selling. I started calling it our "vacation home" to keep things light.

My husband never thought that was funny.

After a couple months of having the house on the market for the fifth time, I was starting to just feel relieved that we didn't have to worry about a renter anymore. I hated the feeling of paying for two houses and coordinating family members to drive by and check on it or mow the lawn for us, but I was thankful someone wasn't tossing a sloppy joe sandwich behind an appliance without my knowledge.

As we approached ninety days of having it listed, we *finally* received an offer. In all the years of listing and renting, I had always imagined the person who would finally buy the house. I just knew that when the buyer presented themselves, it would be some sort of story that all started to make sense. I was convinced it would be a teenage couple who'd had a baby and just gotten married, and that I would be able to compare them to my parents who had been in that same situation. As a result, I would take a low offer. I was ready to cut someone some slack or pay it forward in some way. I was ready for the buyer whose path I was meant to cross.

Our buyer was a weird guy who invested in a lot of properties.

I accepted the offer without negotiating given that he wanted to pay cash and avoid an inspection. He offered $58,000, which seemed painful but joyful all at the same time. His lack of interest in an inspection allowed me to avoid facing the fact that the house still ran on fuses. I was so tired of it all that I simply accepted the offer and waited for the closing day to arrive.

On the day of the closing my husband and I left work early and drove back to Dayton with false expectations about the buyer. I knew he was an investor based on the information my realtor had shared, but I guess I had imagined we would get a group photo or bond over our shared interest in the home.

We walked into the realty office where two men dressed in overly worn T-shirts were placed across the table from us. One was bragging about the number of properties he owned while his flip phone kept ringing in the background. The other kept asking about the keys to the house, *my house*. After twenty-five minutes of signing our names with a slash mark and 532 Clyde

LLC next to it, we were done. We had officially resigned from our jobs as landlords.

I stole their pen and told myself I deserved it.

That was it.

There wasn't a set of teenage parents waiting to go to their new home. There wasn't an elderly lady buying a home that would've made me feel like the house had come full circle. It was simply an investor who would be finding a renter to live in it the following week.

I took a picture with my realtor, congratulated him on his first sale, and we drove back to Columbus with a $58,000 load off our backs.

The following week I went to work and told everyone who had known of the renter sob stories that we had finally sold the house. I still denied that the house ever had bedbugs to the couple people to whom I had previously leaked that information.

I still had an image to uphold.

After two days back at work as the owner of one home instead of two, I received a phone call from an unknown number with the same area code as the city where the house was located. I answered and heard a lady say, "Someone called our office to let us know central air was being installed without the proper permits. Are you the owner of 532 Clyde Place?"

I replied, "Nope."

Brooke Ignet Hocker

DIET STARTS MONDAY

"Just eat your lettuce and be sad." – Lisa Lovely

I CAN'T BE YOUR FRIEND IF you say you love salads. And if you say you love salads *and* you order your salad dressing on the side, you're not even frenemy material. I need to see obvious signs that you battle the bread basket just like me before I can add you to my Christmas gift list.

Every single one of us is fighting this uphill battle to stay "in shape," and it's the worst. Why is it so hard?! I have circled this block so many times that the trip, or "journey" as we like to call it these days, has lost its luster.

My life centered on the sport of gymnastics throughout my entire childhood. Thanks to spending over twenty hours a week in a gym and guidance from my parents on the best food choices, I managed to keep a gymnast-like body until I went to college, *flat chest and all.*

Three weeks into college I made the cheerleading squad. Not only did I pick up where I left off with hours of practice every week, but now I had the luxury of a team trainer who made me lift weights and do cardio before most students were up for class. And let's not forget the obscene amount of miles I had to walk every day as a college student. Life was good. I could eat spaghetti past 8:00 p.m. and didn't even know it was something I should have felt guilty about. I could have my picture taken in a tank top and shorts and didn't have to fear looking like a soccer mom. I could wear a two-piece swimsuit and my only worry was exposing the small hole that was once a belly-button piercing. I even dabbled in protein bars.

After my days of pom-poms ramped down and I became a working adult, I still spent most of my time in the gym. I didn't really know any differently. I gained what I considered to be the normal ten-or-so pounds after college and thought that was what happened when you got a salary and a cubicle. I was still a size 4 (or 2 on a good day), so I had nothing to worry about.

It wasn't too long before Chris and I met, fell in love, and got hitched.

Our meeting was a result of a mutual friend who said we'd make the perfect match. She told Chris she thought we should meet. She told my stepmom to tell me that she thought we should meet. And long story short, once I heard that he "had a broad chest like a bodybuilder," I chose to call him back and meet this fit man who better be husband material.

He *did* have a chest like a bodybuilder. And he *was* a bodybuilder. He had competed in a number of amateur bodybuilding shows, and we spent most of our first date talking about the number of meals he ate in a day. I was fascinated. I wanted to eat a dozen eggs a day and have a fit body and do some sort of fitness-related shows too. *Where do I sign up?*

Nineteen days later I was eating clean. I hadn't even known what that term meant before that moment. I had grown up in a gym, I had always wanted the perfect fit body, I had won a bench press competition in college, I was one of few girls who would actually lift weights in the gym, and now I was googly-eyed over this gorgeous guy who knew everything I needed to know to get me there. Doing sprints at the local track became a good date night for us, and he'd even let me drink water straight from the gallon-sized container he carried everywhere. It was love and I was getting in the best shape of my life.

Love makes you do funny things. When we meet people whom we fall hard for, if they tell us to tattoo our whole face or cut off a limb or sell our house and live in a tent, it would just be a matter of rearranging our work schedule to make it happen. It's a weird love fog. In my case, Chris was already tapping into an interest I had, so we were a match made in grilled chicken breast heaven.

I began eating five meals a day. I began eating vegetables for the first time in my life. I actually touched raw meat and grilled it. I began telling others how they should eat clean because, "You have no idea how good you would feel." (I don't recommend this if you're trying to make new friends). I stopped drinking regular Coke. Every day I carried protein shakers around and packed a cooler large enough for a family picnic. I only talked about working out and figure competitions I was planning to compete in. I kept my blonde highlights fresh at all times and used self-tanning lotion. I was in the best shape of my life and had no idea why other people couldn't do the same. *Didn't they know that if they spent their Sundays cooking food, weighing it out, and putting it in numerous containers, and just spent at least an hour a day at the gym, they could be in the best shape of their lives too?!*

Chris and I got married and life carried on. I started pouring time into getting my Master's degree, and suddenly dinner became a bag of Muddy Buddies Chex Mix. I began giving my career my all and found myself on the receiving end of a string of several promotions over the course of a few years. My cubicle got bigger. So did my ass.

Since then, I've had one foot in the fitness world and one in the carbohydrate world. I've had a series of fitness crazes, like the time I woke up a couple days a week at 5:00 a.m. to go to a spinning class, or when I looked forward all day to going to Zumba. I've started fitness-related Facebook pages for friends and have participated in fitness photo shoots. I've run a couple half marathons and said words only the devil uses as I completed a full marathon.

On the flip side, I've eaten egg whites for dinner followed by donuts for breakfast the next day. I've skipped workouts because I've worked ten-hour work days for a month straight. I've convinced myself that my next meal will be better . . . for thirty-five meals in a row. I am "all in," but less than twelve hours later I'm "all out." I've hidden behind phrases like "balance" and, "It's a lifestyle, not a diet."

On the other hand, Chris has been able to relentlessly keep up with his fitness gig while balancing high work demands. God bless him.

Why is it so hard?! Ladies, I'm talking to you specifically. Why do we start diets every freaking Monday of our lives and find ourselves facedown in a large pizza on a Tuesday, *at lunch nonetheless*. Why do we buy gym passes and expensive pants from lululemon, and then detour so we don't even have to drive by the gym? Why do we only wear workout gear for things like cleaning out the garage or painting a spare bedroom? Why do we all think we need to do some sort of cleanse, like that will wash away twenty-four months of grilled cheese sandwiches and deep-fried anything?! Hell, most of us can't even make our way through an entire cleanse cycle, whatever that means.

In the midst of all our failed attempts, *some* of us do have some moments of success. We're not all failures *all the time*. We do find a magic diet that works for us for the moment, or a workout that we become slightly addicted to for a couple months, or we find supplements that we think are helping us lose weight and we consider becoming a distributor.

I'm convinced there are six triggers in this life that get us motivated enough to actually pack our lunches or do squats:

1. We're on the dating scene. There is nothing in this world that will motivate us more than those first eight weeks of dating someone new. We will change our entire lives around to look our best in the hopes that this person will be in awe of us. I can always tell when someone I work with is dating someone new because they've never looked better. This

method normally ends with a long-term relationship and the reappearance of those twenty pounds you thought you'd never see again.

2. We're jealous. Few motivating factors rival the need for pure vengeance that comes with being jealous of a friend, colleague, or some cute fitness star of a girl you saw talking to your husband once at the gym (a *totally* random example). "Oh, just wait, you, in your size small workout gear and perfect ponytail. You think *you're* in good shape?!" can push any woman to the brink, even to a point where they give up white bread and chocolate when they have PMS, just out of a pure "I'll show you" motivation. This method normally ends with a grand entrance at an event where you wear uncomfortable high heels and a brand new, overpriced dress just to prove a point.

3. We've had a health scare. One of the purest forms of motivation can come from a health scare, be it our own health scare or observations of a family member going through a medical scare so large that we decide to change our lives for the better. This method is most likely to stick for the long-term.

4. We need to control something. It's been said that eating disorders are rooted in control issues. I'm no expert on eating disorders, but

the ability to control anything you or your family eats when you feel a loss of control seems to make sense. This method normally ends in a lifetime of struggle fed by positive reinforcement from strangers.

5. We want revenge. Upon a long and dramatic breakup, we spend our time getting into the best shape of our lives for pure revenge. We channel anger and listen to old Alanis Morissette or Destiny's Child songs while we start new things like boxing or running outside. We go on the South Beach Diet and start eating a diet made up of only 30 percent complex carbohydrates. This method normally ends in "unplanned" public run-ins with an ex and an overabundance of selfies from bars (See also: The Divorce Diet.)

6. We're going on vacation. I've never understood vacation diets. So, you're dieting for a vacation where you're going to see a bunch of people you'll never see again, plus the people you live with have already seen you at your worst? Tell me again what's motivating you in that situation? This method normally ends with too many margaritas and high chances of dehydration.

No matter what motivational method you are or aren't following, what I have learned is that nobody can talk you into wanting to get into shape. You're either feelin' it or you're not. If you're not ready to go all in, then you're going to go half-ass in and convince yourself that you can't do it because the healthy food in your refrigerator will spoil while you eat chips and salsa for your best friend's birthday *even though you swore you wouldn't eat them.*

I believe health needs to be our priority in life, and not just physical health, but mental as well. I wholeheartedly believe that if our mental state of mind is healthy, then we'd be better prepared to make our physical self match. Find someone who is depressed and it's highly likely you're not finding them in the gym or the produce aisle at Whole Foods.

I'm guessing I will have another season of life where I'm in the best shape I'll ever be in, though it feels so far away sometimes. I will probably then leave that season for cinnamon rolls and pizza, only to return again when my mind is right again.

Until then, here's to starting over on Monday.

PSYCHIC CINDY

"No use borrowing trouble" – *Lisa Lovely*

I THINK WE ALL DESIRE TO know what our futures will hold. Anyone who tells you otherwise is lying. According to a sketchy website that forced me to the App Store to purchase suspicious apps, psychic services is a $2 billion per year industry. I'm not sure how they're calculating these numbers because my gut tells me psychics aren't reporting accurate income on their taxes, *but what do I know?* I just know that every time I've gone to see a psychic, there's been specific instruction to pay with cash. That's not to say psychics aren't tracking my payment in an Excel spreadsheet somewhere behind their crystal balls and incense paraphernalia, but I'm still skeptical about how finance experts arrived at that number.

This $2 billion industry includes 1-900 numbers

people still have on speed dial. Did we learn nothing from the Miss Cleo lawsuit? It also includes services such as palm reading, ghost-busting, tarot card reading, aura reading, channeling spirits, astrology counsel, numerology, and dream interpretations. I even read online that psychics report seeing an increase in business when the economy suffers. *We can't pay our forty-five-dollar electric bills, but we sure can scrounge up fifty-five dollars for a psychic reading to find out if we'll be able to pay said electric bill.*

I've always been fascinated with the idea of psychics. I don't believe in ghosts or spirits though, mainly because I'm scared of the dark and have told myself they don't exist so I can sleep at night when my husband is out of town. Or when I walk upstairs by myself even when he is in town.

My mom has a similar fascination with the whole psychic thing too. We shared a casual interest in shows like *Long Island Medium* or *Crossing Over* in the past, and I remember her telling me several stories about friends who had visited palm readers and everything they were told came true—of course. I'm convinced everyone knows someone who went to a psychic and their life unfolded exactly as predicted. As a result, most of us are left straddling the line between reading our horoscope every day and claiming psychic services are sacrilege.

Now, I'm a Christian. I pray a lot, I love praise songs and sing them terribly, I surround myself with strong Christian friends, I talk about and to God often, and I make conservative choices that match the Christian stereotype. I don't read the Bible except once per year when I get the overwhelming sensation to open it (only to realize I don't understand anything in it). We don't go to church because we find other, less important excuses like its distance from our house, or we have to catch up on work, or we have to work out, or we feel straight with God even though we don't show up on Sundays unless a niece is getting baptized or a friend is performing the music. But I am a Christian, and it's a very important part of my life.

I don't know God's stance on psychics, fortune-tellers, palm readers, readers of auras, and sketchy characters alike, but I'm guessing there's a verse or two in the ol' Bible that wouldn't support such activities. So I participate in these events with an "I'm a Christian, I don't really believe in this, I don't believe in ghosts either, it's just for fun" attitude.

I mean, I believe them if the news is good. I disdain them if the news is bad. I pay them either way.

———

Psychic Sue

During a summer in my college years, when every student would pay anyone fifty dollars to tell them what their future holds, my friend Jen and I had our hearts set on going to a psychic. Coincidentally, the ever-so-famous and hilarious TV show *Will and Grace* had just aired the "Gypsies, Tramps and Weed" episode. Will (Eric McCormack) uses a birthday gift certificate from Grace (Debra Messing) for a psychic consultation with "Psychic Sue" (Camryn Manheim). All of Psychic Sue's predictions for Will's life become true over twenty-three minutes and a few commercial breaks.

Clearly, psychics are real.

Jen and I were determined to find our Psychic Sue to learn who we would marry, how many kids we would have, and what our future careers would be so we'd know if we should change our majors. We looked up psychics in the Dayton, Ohio area—not a booming city for the psychic business—and found one who was close enough for comfort but far enough away from our small-town suburb. We were so nervous that we began laughing and squealing and saying a lot of phrases that started with, "Oh my gosh" as we headed to a part of town known for its gentlemen's clubs.

I think it's fairly common to get nervous before seeing a psychic. It's one of those moments where you start asking yourself what you really believe in and question what your family would think of you if they knew you went. You'll never care more about what your Grandma thinks of you until you're at an ATM asking yourself if you should withdraw forty or sixty dollars while pondering if a tip is standard psychic service protocol.

After driving past the destination three times, Jen and I finally arrived at our Psychic Sue's. Her name wasn't Sue, but that's what we would call her for all of eternity. Psychic Sue had a home-based business— you know, because that's where her spirit guides lived and stuff. As we pulled into the gravel driveway, we parked right behind one of those vans that had curtains on the windows and a mural spray-painted on the side. It was the kind of van you're positive a hippie, or a man who lures kids in with suckers and candies, lives in. I spent most of my elementary school years learning to resist men and their suckers if they're in those scary vans, (even though I have yet to see a news story that actually starts with a man and a cherry blow pop), and here I was parking behind the scary-sucker-man-mural-painted van in my 1996 white Sunfire with my bestie riding shotgun.

Everything our parents taught us not to do, we were doing, and we had cash.

The readings went down in the side part of the house. We entered through one of those rooms where you're unclear if it's an addition, an awkward sunroom, or a garage converted to a tiny apartment for an estranged brother who'd had to move in with them. We sat in a small and cluttered waiting area with furniture similar to that of the local funeral home and yellow-stained art on the walls as a finishing touch, the best of which included a picture of Jesus, Amen.

As we got squirmy in the waiting area, we justified our visit and our ticket into heaven with comments like, "I mean, she has The Last Supper painting hanging up. She has to be legit." I guess we thought that was a sign that God himself had employed her to tap into spirits he would be providing. The painting somehow gave her credibility that she could give two twenty-something-year-olds insight into their future lives as wives, mothers, and professionals working in a field they didn't even know they were interested in.

We had both arrived in hopes of getting our (*sweaty*) palms read. I even stared at my palms before we arrived as if to memorize which lines were deeper than others to see if I could magically tell how many kids I would have, how many near-death experiences I would face, and the length of my life line. I had spent several hours in local book stores flipping through palm reading and astrology books, which I felt had practically qualified me to do the job myself.

Psychic Sue eventually called us back one at a time while the other person (*sucker*) sat with her ear against the door. We were both disappointed to find out she would not be reading our palms that day but rather reading our auras per her spirit guides' recommendation. I wasn't sure what an aura was exactly, but I did know that I had just paid a lady twenty dollars to tell me I was surrounded by the color blue.

She also asked me my favorite destination, to which I said "Florida" because I couldn't think of anything better. (*I hate heat, why did I say Florida?!*) She told me the color blue symbolized good energy, that I would eventually move to Florida (*Where did she come up with that location?!*), and that I would wear a white coat in my future job (*So I should change to pre-med?*). I left there imagining how proud my parents would be of my future as a doctor and hoped they would forget about the part of town I'd had to travel to for that information.

———

Renaissance Palm Reader

A few years post-Psychic Sue, I went to the Renaissance Festival with my mom. We're not the people who dress the part and talk with the accent, but we do enjoy buying overpriced Renaissance jewelry while eating two bites of gigantic turkey legs that cost us twelve dollars.

After roaming the scene for a couple hours, we

passed a carriage with a sign for a palm reader on our way out. We instantly glanced at the sign, then glanced at each other, and then glanced at the sign again in perfect synchronization. The carriage looked like Professor Marvel's (Frank Morgan) from *The Wizard of Oz*, one of our favorite movies. Not paying whoever was inside who knew the secrets of our futures wasn't an option at this point.

Without debate, we dug into our purses to see how much cash we had left. The excitement of finding the carriage and discovering our futures faded fast as we continued to wait an obnoxious amount of time for our turns in the carriage. It got to a point where we not only didn't want to go into the carriage anymore, but we didn't even want to be at the fair anymore. My mom gave some "Geez, what's taking so long?" looks my way while I tried to give the "It'll be fun" look back as I sat in the summer heat on a bale of hay sweating—and regretting the turkey leg.

The palm reader proved to be a creepy guy with long hair and disgustingly long nails.

Twenty dollars later, I found out that I didn't like being in small carriages by myself with creepy men with long nails, I was an overall happy person, and I would move to Florida someday (*really, Florida, again?*). I left feeling slightly violated because the creepy man had held my hand the entire time while he predicted my future.

That was the last time we ever visited the Renaissance Festival.

———

Carnival Fortune-Teller

In 2013, a carnival-themed summer meeting had been planned for my department at work. This was the kind of meeting where we spent the equivalent of one person's salary on catered food and organized team-building. In the weeks leading up to the event, I jokingly told the coworker coordinating the festivities that I would not attend unless she booked a palm reader. It just seemed appropriate given the theme. Secretly, I would've settled for the Smallest Pony in the World or a bearded lady, but requesting a fortune-teller and threatening not to attend seemed way more fun.

On the day of the meeting, also known as the hottest day in the world, I shuffled around to each carnival-themed activity with my assigned group. There were bouncy-house types of games, some sort of child-like archery game, and other various activities that required us to take our shoes off. One by one, people were getting injured, twisting ankles, and throwing their shoulders out of socket. As I moved to the last rotation of activities, I was shocked and excited to see a fortune-teller! I had gotten my wish! All I wanted was for my injured and sweaty coworkers to get out of the way so I could find out my life's destiny. I was the one who'd requested this palm reader, so I deserved to go first.

No one else knew I had requested the palm reader for the work party, so no one else cared about making sure I got to go first. I stood in line for far too long, but *clearly* this lady sitting at a fold-out table in the middle of a field in hundred-degree weather knew what my life and three hundred of my closest coworkers' lives had in store. She even had an assistant. I wasn't about to pass up the opportunity despite the line and the heat. After losing five pounds of sweat and discussing if psychics were real or not with the people next to me in line, it was *finally* my turn.

I did what I imagine everyone does when they go to a psychic. I approached this Goddess of the Future in a stiff way so as to not give away any traits about myself. I was testing her spirit-guided knowledge. I hid my wedding band and pretended to be an introvert, as if introverts go to psychics. Like Psychic Sue and the creepy Renaissance palm reader, I was testing her from the minute I laid eyes on her—and her unwashed hair.

Very quickly after sitting down, I flipped my palm and she began to tell me "secrets" about my life. These "secrets" were general statements:

"You're outgoing." *Okay lady, you obviously saw me socializing with all the other fools in line.*

"You sometimes compromise yourself to make others happy." *Okay, perhaps.*

"You're . . . Have you ever been pregnant?"

I was thirty-one-years old at the time with a couple therapy sessions under my belt to sort through my feelings about ever wanting a baby someday. The answer was no, but if she would've pulled out a couch and let me kick my feet up then I could've shared all my hopes and dreams and fears about the topic.

I give a quick no.

"Soooo . . . you haven't had a miscarriage?"

As she spoke, a bell rang.

It was not the type of bell that signified an angel getting its wings. As a matter of fact, wings were probably falling off of angels as the reading was happening.

I was confused by her question but quickly realized the assistant's main responsibility: to abruptly hit the bell just as the crisis-type information was delivered. The fortune-teller handed me her business card. "Oh, well, then I wouldn't worry about it."

I wouldn't worry about it?!

You mean the single hardest decision for me to make in my life? The topic of long, drawn-out conversations with my husband late at night when no serious conversation should ever happen? You mean the biggest pending question I have in my life? You wouldn't worry about it?! Not only do I have to figure out if I want to be a mom someday, but now I have to live with nonchalant miscarriage statements by a lady on a folding chair with hair that hasn't been washed since 1992?!

Who requested a fortune-teller anyway?

I stood up and returned to my coworkers. The eager looks on their faces to hear the verdict made me quickly realize I shouldn't share the news about her "non-worrisome" miscarriage statement. I decided to go with, "She nailed it," followed by some laughs while I shared generic statements about having positive energy and a great personality that I figured everyone would receive.

During post-worst-fortune-teller-reading-ever, I learned from a coworker that she had a go-to psychic. She used phrases that started with, "My psychic," indicating she had been multiple times. Another coworker, Cindy, and I were loving everything we heard about this person's psychic. She told us about the readings she had received and how she herself had some psychic abilities that her psychic had helped her hone and develop. Cindy and I decided right there in the hot temperatures and the secret scares of a miscarriage that we must immediately make appointments for this person's psychic.

The next day at work we ditched doing anything productive for our jobs. Cindy made appointments for us to see the referral psychic, whose name was, ironically, Cindy.

Psychic Cindy

I did what all friends of people making psychic appointments for them do: I bombarded her with questions. "What information did you give the psychic?" "Does she have your full name?" "Did you tell her my name?" "Did you give her just my first name or my last name too?" Realistically (as if we're discussing reality), any psychic running a shop where appointments are required in advance can gather all key facts from social media.

I had watched a news story on TV the previous year where psychic readings were being offered in New York City, and the only requirement to get the reading was providing your full name. The psychic proceeded to tell people all kinds of facts that had proven to be real events in their lives. The person running the event then revealed a screen that had their Facebook feed behind it with pictures of them doing the very events the psychic had just shared. *Were these people that stupid? Am I that stupid?* Given the requirement for appointments ahead of time, I figured the chances were high that Psychic Cindy would know I just scored a trench coat at GAP for fourteen dollars and that I had a newfound love for pour-over coffee.

The days leading up to the appointment were nonproductive as far as our jobs went, but totally productive in reading Psychic Cindy's website and gambling on the fifty-fifty chance that her website may give us a computer virus. Similar to *The Last Supper* justification at "Psychic Sue's," I started justifying this appointment based on the fact that she advertised herself as an author and life coach. *She had to be legit if she's coaching people through life, right?* According to the clip art on her website, she also doubled as a ghostbuster should someone have a spirit haunting them which they'd like exterminated. I couldn't get over the thought of her looking up clip art options that best represented her ability to get rid of ghosts.

When the psychic appointment day finally arrived, my friend Cindy left work and headed to her appointment while I trailed behind her by about twenty minutes. I told everyone I knew on the way out of the office that I was headed to see a psychic. Everyone was intrigued and entertained and some begged me to invite them the next time. I hadn't really considered the need for a "next time," *assuming I was going to make it out alive,* because I expected she would be telling me my entire future in one sitting. A psychic visit is meant to be more of a one-night stand as far as I'm concerned.

I put the address of the office (I had upgraded to psychics in real offices) in Google Maps and headed on my way. I felt nervous. When I arrived, I looked up to find her office was located across the street from the therapist I saw during the decide-if-I-want-a-baby-someday phase. I found irony in it and thought God was playing a trick on me. I began to wonder if God was putting bad checkmarks by my name in his book of people who are supposed to go to heaven. I didn't think God had really done that, but I didn't know what I thought anymore.

I drove slowly to the back of what appeared to be a mix of Florida-like condos and business offices. *Was this the "Florida" the other psychics had predicted?* It was a set of buildings that looked like either an iguana should run by your feet or twenty-seven psychologists and an acupuncturist should save people from emotional and physical pain.

I walked into the office lobby where suddenly all of the furniture felt small and I felt huge. No one was there. It was me, a spread of meditative and psychic journals, semi-perfect lighting if it had been a little darker outside, the faint smell of incense, and ten different business cards for everyone who worked there ("worked" being a loose term in my opinion), ranging from psychics to spiritual healers to hypnotists to people who did trance work, *whatever that is.*

I took a seat and sent a text message to my husband, Chris, that included the address with, "Just in case I get killed here, this is where I am." He responded, "Get out of there."

I glanced behind me and found an Audi in the parking lot with a personalized license plate that said "ONENESS." I convinced myself it was Psychic Cindy's car. Chris had been researching Audis for over a year and I couldn't help but wonder if Psychic Cindy's career choice brought in more income than mine and Chris's combined.

I slid my hand into my purse to confirm I had

enough cash on me. Psychic Cindy had quoted us fifty-five dollars, which was much higher than Psychic Sue, the creepy Renaissance palm reader, and the free carnival fortune-teller. I multiplied fifty-five dollars by thirty minutes by the number of people she could see in a day by the number of weeks in a year.

That was definitely Psychic Cindy's Audi.

I started to get an unsettling feeling in my stomach and wondered if it was all worth it.

I knew I would get thirty minutes for my fifty-five dollars, but I began fretting about what to ask during that time. Was this going to be a situation where I think she's reading my palm but really she's going to pull an aura-reading stunt like so many sketchy psychics had done before? Was I supposed to ask her about what the other fortune-teller lady had said about a miscarriage? Did she know that fortune-teller? Did everyone in the psychic business know each other? *Were psychics even real?*

After an awkward seventeen-minute wait, friend Cindy and Psychic Cindy appeared from around the corner. They hugged. Friend Cindy looked at me, smiled, said, "I'll talk to you later," and was gone like the wind. I wanted to puke and high-five her all at the same time.

Psychic Cindy greeted me with gigantic eyes as I looked her over. I was looking for signs of the supernatural, that she had been born with a super-secret ability no one else had that would be visible by a diamond or jewel buried somewhere in her skin. Instead, she was a skinny lady with blonde hair who was very nice and made good (almost too good) eye contact. She said, "If you're ready, come on back," as if there were additional prep I needed to do other than wonder about the lives and stories of the two people I'd seen walk in and out of the door while I was in the lobby.

She took me down the longest hallway ever. I knew that friend Cindy had made it out alive, but now I doubted where that hallway was leading and if all these so-called "psychics" have discussions about offices and rental space and contracts and real-world stuff. I assumed they had to in order to sign contracts on office buildings, but did they have team meetings like people in "normal" jobs do?

We finally arrived at her office, or space, *or cave*. I could not have found my way back to the lobby or my car if my life depended on it, and I thought my life might depend on it based on what was going to happen in the next thirty minutes.

Her office felt like a combination of a University professor's office mixed with a massage therapist's room mixed with a senior living facility living room. She had a massage table, a bookshelf, and a little stand that looked like a TV tray.

I sat on the couch and did an internal self-assessment. *Of course she knows I'm a working professional based on my outfit, and of course she knows I'm married based on my ring.* Outside of the giveaways, I was told from friend Cindy that Psychic Cindy only had my first name. I was convinced she had looked up friend Cindy's LinkedIn profile, had seen I was one of her connections, and likely read my profile in advance.

Since I hadn't had a chance to consult with friend Cindy on how her meeting all went down, I was getting anxious in my seat while wondering what the next thirty minutes would bring. Psychic Cindy asked me what I'd like to get out of my time with her, so I came up with something on the fly.

"Well, I guess if you could tell me what the next five years will look like, that would be great."

A genius answer I had not pre-planned, but it seemed to serve as the perfect intro. Psychic Cindy thought it was genius too because she said, "Wow, I really liked the way you phrased that."

I then decided I liked her and she could do no wrong. My ego was also inflating at the same rate her spirit guides were entering the conversation.

She was complimenting me and giving me creepy eye contact while shuffling tarot cards. *Perfect. A prop! Now I won't have to worry about coming up with questions or showing her my sweaty palms and revealing that I still bite the skin around my nails even at age thirty-one.*

She pulled the TV-tray-looking thing in between us and said she would use the tarot cards to show me the next five years. I was hoping God didn't hate me at this point while I scooted forward on the couch to see these magical cards.

She made five rows with the cards, one for each year, and laid a long line of cards in vertical rows underneath each one. I hoped this exercise would fill the entire thirty minutes.

She closed her eyes, took a deep breath in, and said, "Okay, guys. Help me out here."

I instantly disliked her and felt scared.

She told me she was talking to her spirit guides. I didn't know these spirit guides personally, but her tone seemed a little bully-ish when she spoke to them. She would stop in between delivering the news of my future over the course of the thirty minutes to say things like, "Okay, guys. I'll tell her. Fine."

I wanted to yell at the spirit guides and tell them to

go away, and I wanted this lady to just take my fifty-five dollars. Hell, she could've taken my whole purse. I just wanted to flee the scene.

I clutched my purse tightly as she started with the current year, 2013. She said, "Have you just completed some sort of certification or something?"

I thought for a few minutes and said, "Oh, actually, I just finished my MBA."

"Really?! Okay, see!" She responded cheerfully, as if she were impressed with herself.

I was a little impressed too. I loosened the grip on my purse.

She glanced down at the cards and told me the rest of 2013 would be great and proceeded with some filler information and mumbo jumbo about having good energy.

She moved on to 2014 and told me that she saw a job change: specifically, a director position and something having to do with operations. She had hit the sweet spot for an overly ambitious thirty-something-year-old woman without kids and too much focus on her career. I was in the thick of moving my career forward and totally consumed with finding my next position and campaigning for a promotion. I told her the details of how I was in an operations role but had been interviewing for director positions. She told me the position I was interviewing for at the time was not the right one, but that I would be in a director position by April or May of 2015. I was pleased with the news and started to wonder if maybe I should give her a tip in addition to the fee when it was over.

She then slid her hand over to the 2015 stack. At this point, I didn't know if the images on the cards were driving her statements, if she was making this stuff up, or if the so-called spirit guides were still at the party, but I knew I was getting promoted and I didn't care from whom that information was coming. She said 2015 would be a materialistic year.

I'll take it. I began dreaming of me and Chris swimming in seas of money with our only concerns and conversations centered on what home renovation or car we should purchase next.

By the time she got to the 2016 section of cards, she told me I would be happy (as if promotions and cold hard cash weren't enough). She told me that I would begin to have a lot of autonomy in my role (*I tried to remember the definition of autonomy*). She even showed me a card that had a picture of a person holding a book as she said, "See, that's you with a book."

I have always wanted to write a book. It was like she could see into my soul.

Still on the 2016 line of cards, she stopped and said, "I'm getting the feeling you don't have kids?"

I was feeling so good about my future at this point, I took that as a compliment to my body shape and workouts and less to my overall look that resembles a twelve-year-old. I confirmed her suspicions as she said, "I see a child in 2016."

I decided I was okay with that news and wondered if I should've skipped seeing the therapist across the street and just gone straight to Psychic Cindy the whole time.

Then she dropped a spirit-guide-directed bombshell.

She said, "But I do see the loss of your first one."

What?! Loss? Are you freaking serious right now Psychic

Cindy?

I was in shock. I was so immersed in the reading at this point I said, "Actually, I just went to something at work where a lady was reading palms (that sounded better than, "I begged a coworker to bring a fortune-teller to a carnival we had"), and the palm reader asked if I'd had a miscarriage." Psychic Cindy reassured (and scared) me that now since I'd heard that message from both of them, then it was more likely to be true.

I hated my life and that imposter Florida office.

She moved to the 2017 line as I sat there scarred from the news of 2016. She repeated things about my good energy and great life and then she flipped a card that said "fertility" on it. It was not like the other cards that had weird images of kings and swords and horses and random things that made no sense on them. That was the only card with a word printed on it. She said that I would have a baby during 2017 after a long time of trying. The next card she showed me had four hands holding up goblet glasses making a toast, which apparently symbolized the celebration of the new life.

I was stunned. The reading was so specific. I cringed to think about how I would feel if it all came true. And we still had ten minutes to spare.

She asked me if I had any other questions for her during our time. She and her spirit guides had pretty much covered the basics, so I began scrambling for ways to fill the time. I was getting promoted, spending a lot of money, holding a book that I was imagining that I had written, and having a baby. Was there more to life to ask about?

I asked her if she could tell me the gender of the

baby I would have in 2017. As good as her and her spirit guides were, I guess gender identity isn't in their repertoire. She told me she couldn't tell me that information, and I started to realize the reading may all have been a hoax, *except the part where she could see into my soul and invisible spirits were telling her my future with such certainty.*

I decided to use the final minutes to ask about my parents. As the words, "What about the health of my parents?" came out of my mouth, I instantly regretted it. *If this so-called ghost-busting life coach, author, spiritual guide, and psychic Reiki Master even thinks of telling me one of my parents will get sick, I will lose it, flip her massage table over, and walk in circles in the long hallway* (because I would've never found the lobby again in that weird building).

She asked my mom's name and wrote it down in her journal. I felt uncomfortable, like I had just given away my mom's identity and thought Psychic Cindy would use that information to open illegal credit cards under her name.

She closed her eyes as if to channel my mother from an hour-and-a-half down Interstate 70, where she lived. I wondered if my mom knew it was happening while it went on.

"Your mom is healthy, but I see something in her lungs, like she's breathing in something she shouldn't be breathing in."

I found myself saying, "Well, she *does* go to the casino a lot and there's smoke in there."

Psychic Cindy replied, "Have her check the carbon monoxide detectors in her house."

I got excited about the specific instructions because there was such certainty in her predictions. I almost hoped my mom's carbon monoxide detectors were broken (but that she was still healthy of course!)

She asked my dad's name but must've channeled him much more quickly because she didn't write his name down in her journal.

At least I wouldn't have to explain why his identity was stolen too.

She told me he's in overall good health, and I was relieved that I didn't have to wrestle with telling him some sort of bad news that a so-called psychic had told me about him for a mere fifty-five dollars.

The session came to a close and I pulled cash out of my wallet. She hugged me.

I hoped God still loved me.

———

Following this ten-year-long tour of sporadic psychic visits, life delivered what Psychic Cindy and her spirit guides had promised.

Two weeks after the Psychic Cindy visit, my mom forwarded an email to me that all employees at her company had received: their building would be closed over the weekend so they could complete a process to filter the air in the building as it was causing some to become sick.

Six months later, friend Cindy received a job offer in California, packed up, and hit the road. As a result, I got promoted to her job: director.

A year-and-a-half later, when our materialistic year arrived, I hit a jackpot on a slot machine in Las Vegas and was greeted by casino attendants with $20,206.27 in cold hard cash.

In late 2015, I began writing a book.

As for kids, I'm still in therapy.

Do What I Say

Brooke Ignet Hocker

ACKNOWLEDGEMENTS

Thank you to my husband, Chris Hocker, for the unconditional and relentless love and support around my dreams of becoming a writer. Thank you for letting this book take over my thoughts, conversations, and weekends. Thank you for listening to me every time I gave a recap of all the chapters and my feelings on every word I had written that day. Thank you for traveling to New York City with me so I could attend a writers conference even though you prefer mountains and camping and playing in the woods. I love you.

Thank you to one of my best friends, Angela Heck Mueller, for going all in on our Gals with Goals blog. Thanks for believing in me and building my confidence up every time I have doubted myself. Thank you for reading the essays that make up this book and calling me at 8:00 a.m. on a Saturday to give me feedback and squeal in excitement. Thank you for dinners that turn into four hours of good conversation.

Thank you to my Grandmothers for letting me talk non-stop for hours on end, always. Thank you to my Grandma Dona for sharing your humor and love of writing with me. Thank you to my Grandma Linda for being such a loving and gentle person and encouraging me every step of the way no matter what I get myself into.

Thank you to my childhood besties, Molly Stull and Matt Barhorst, for voluntarily serving as my first round of editors. Thank you for living these stories with me and taking the time to catch every grammatical error I had to offer.

Thank you to my tiny entourage, my blog readers, for keeping me going and taking an interest in my life adventures.

Thank you to the New York Writers Workshop for giving me the confidence to declare myself a real writer.

Thank you to editor, Blake Atwood, for saving me, this book, and its readers from hundreds of pages of numbers that were supposed to be spelled out, an overabundance of commas, curse words that were awkwardly inserted, and a handful of semicolons when I felt like it made a sentence look cool. Your attention to detail and talent has been the cherry on top of this creation.

Thank you to my favorite place in Columbus, Fox in the Snow Café, for not only providing a beautiful place for me to write, but for feeding me the best cinnamon rolls in the city that resulted in a series of diets throughout the creation of this book.

Thank you to my stepparents, sister, extended family, in-laws, friends, and readers. You make my life full of love, support, and laughs.

Thank you to my parents for being the most amazing people on the planet. Thank you for your ongoing humor and guidance for which none of this would be possible without. Thank you for being real, honest, and providing the best advice that is the basis of my life and this book.

Brooke Ignet Hocker